D0928076

6 DEC 2016
Lily

②

THE MIDDLE AGES

L n pes se tient e pacience
H e remaundit grundit ne rece
V n de ses clers li dub bel sire
C u musz bad iun martire
F u traite hui de cuncorde
K e a la uerite se acorde
K ar par martire ert faite
B ien le uif deun finie
P ar uile mort sentre iglise
C unquerra pes e franchise
L arceuesq̄ a co respunt
L o plesse a deu ki suble mund
P ur sa tīe seure ꝑ⁊⁊
⁊ ꝑ tut sun regne cūstiner
S un fiz bert eir a Wemuns
h eurt li roit uiert cōrunes
d ies plusur tut ꝭ greues
⁊ ꝭ uiurendre e entanues
L a bonure e la franchise
d l arceuesq̄ e sa iglise
G rant gent reidoit barue
D e clerge e de cheualerie

L i rois henri grante e dune
D e engleterre la curune
A sun fiz esne henri
R epentant fu puis e marri
L i prelat deuerbie roger
A tort leinpust a turuper
R oger deuerbie isu
L i arceuesq̄ cuneu
L euesq̄ fu de lundres la
E ist de ꝭecestre iua
L i euesq̄ de salesbure
C untre lorin de canterebure
Q ue larceuesq̄ cist tut tort
F urent a corouer le roi
h enri le iosne las liue
ꝙ ur en auiur mesquenture
a feste sunt plenerement
d u mang curent giaunt gent
L e pere fist aufiz giaunt feste
H e oimes en chantun nen geste
K i fust de riche hom seruir
C um fu li iosne rois henri

L i pere⁊ li fiz ioie si grant
K a ceu uir li fu sergaunt
C oianz plusurs gei
K e sul fu uis iosne henri
R e ceu eist ki dune seruir
D unt mut apres se repenti
ꝙ ur sendolut en apres
K ar poi dura laūur e pes
A pres poi dure sen dilirt
K il auꝑe guerre mut
C o fu au cumencement
L e p̄mer entuchement
D u perche lu roi henri
K i seruir thomas tant pur sun
baru li plat de canterebure
L oi reumter e diue
ꝙ ur se tuit despersone
E mut sun honur blesce
L a dignete de sa iglise
ꝙ ur desrumdbre e maūuise
A ser les enfū chastier
E par la pape amonestez

A ROYAL HISTORY OF ENGLAND

THE MIDDLE AGES

BY JOHN GILLINGHAM
AND PETER EARLE

EDITED BY
ANTONIA FRASER

CASSELL&CO

First published in the United Kingdom in 2000 by Cassell & Co

The text of *The Middle Ages* is taken from the single-volume
The Lives of the Kings & Queens of England, first published in the United
Kingdom in 1975 by Weidenfeld & Nicolson, revised in 1993 and 1998.

Text copyright © Cassell & Co 2000
Design and layout copyright © Cassell & Co 2000

All rights reserved. No part of this publication may be reproduced
in any material form (including photocopying or storing it in any medium by
electronic means and whether or not transiently or incidentally to some other
use of this publication) without the written permission of the copyright
owner, except in accordance with the provisions of the Copyright, Designs
and Patents Act 1988 or under the terms of a licence issued by the Copyright
Licensing Agency, 90 Tottenham Court Road, London W1P 9HE.
Applications for the copyright owner's permission to reproduce any
part of this publication should be addressed to the publisher.

A CIP catalogue record for this book is available
from the British Library.

ISBN 0304355402

Jacket images: front © Weidenfeld & Nicolson Archives (Isabella of France,
wife of Edward II, entering Bath); back © The Bridgeman Art Library,
London (the murder of Thomas Becket, Archbishop of Canterbury, 29
December 1170, from a thirteenth-century book of psalms).

Endpapers: Illuminated manuscript of Richard the Lionheart departing
for the Third Crusade in 1190, from the Chronicle of David Aubert.
Page 2: The coronation of the Young King, Henry II's eldest son, from
Vie de St Thomas, written in England in the mid-thirteenth century.

Cassell & Co
Wellington House
125 Strand
London WC2R 0BB

CONTENTS

INTRODUCTION

The Middle Ages – and 'English history' – are held to begin with an alien invasion and a famous date: the defeat of Harold Godwinesson by William the Conqueror at Hastings in 1066. On this day, England came under the sway of the Norman Kings, and the long-beleagured island was transformed into an unassailable fortress. Norman rule saw the evolution of the first governmental institutions of the modern state: notably the Curia Regis from which a parliamentary assembly would derive and a strong hereditary monarchy.

Yet medieval records are so few that the personalities of England's Norman sovereigns, ruling at a time when a monarch's actions were decisive in shaping the course of events, remain shadowy and insubstantial. What does emerge, however, is that those who presided over this remarkable period were not figures of nobility, let alone chivalry.

William I was a brutal, enormous man who captured England against what seemed impossible odds, as much by ruthless will as by good luck and the weakness of his enemies. His third son, William Rufus (William II) suffered from the combined defects of an evil temper, an unattractive, ruddy appearance (hence the nickname) and a stutter. Killed whilst out hunting one day (accident or murder?) his brother, Henry, seized the opportunity and was crowned three days later.

Henry I, the 'Lion of Justice', promised his subjects good government and loyalty. More of a diplomat and the most distinguished of the lot, Henry did much for the reformation of English law and government. The issue of his succession, however, proved controversial and his imposition of his daughter, Matilda, instead of her cousin, Stephen, upon the Curia Regis as successor engendered anarchic rivalry and civil disorder.

It was, however, Stephen who was crowned in 1135. A likeable but ineffective monarch, peace came only when he accepted to adopt Matilda's son, Henry, as his heir. Together with his formidable wife, Eleanor of Aquitaine, Henry II governed the magnificent Angevin Empire from 1154–89. An advocate for rational reform, Henry overhauled the judicial system and lay the foundations of English common law. But he is perhaps best known for one of the most famous quarrels in history: one that resulted in the murder of his 'turbulent priest', Thomas Becket.

Of all the medieval kings, the reign of Richard I, Henry's third son, belongs in myth. For most of us, this crusading king belongs to a pantheon that includes King Arthur and Robin Hood. In an ironic twist, his brother 'Bad King John', is equally as legendary, but his story is one that dies hard in British history. Just as every schoolchild has heard of the Magna Carta, the character of the monarch from whom these concessions were wrung by righteous barons has been unfairly blackened.

John's son, Henry III, was famously described by Dante as 'the simple king who sat apart' even though it is Henry to whom we are indebted for his patronage of the arts and commitment to the enhancement of English civilisation. But, labelled as pious and indolent, he is often glossed over by historians in favour of his heroic son, Edward. In an age of troubadours and tournaments, castles and crusades, Edward I was lauded as 'the best lance in all the world'.

In contrast, the life of Edward II has all the elements of drama and inclines one to wonder and pity. Surely the heir of the mighty Edward I was set for success and glory? Edward II succeeded to the throne in 1307 at the age of twenty-three, but twenty years later his reign, punctuated by rebellion and civil war, plus a disastrous love affair with a young squire, ended in an enforced abdication and a cruel and ignominious death.

Edward III, another unlikely son, is best known for his great self-confidence and ability to work with the English nation as a whole. It is to him that we look for the growth of English nationalism, the fame of England abroad and the exact relationship and division of authority between King and Parliament.

The Plantagenet dynasty – sometimes called the Devil's Brood because they were said to be condemned to fight each other – closes with the tragic reign of Richard II. Richard was deposed from the throne of England by his cousin Henry Bolingbroke in 1399 – the future Henry IV – who won the crown seeking vengeance for his banishment. Bolingbroke may have been crowned king, but the vexed question of his claim to the throne and the issue of his succession precipitated the quarrel between the Houses of York and Lancaster in the next century: a battle for the crown which was to become known as the Wars of the Roses, and which was not resolved until the establishment of the Tudor dynasty in 1485.

Dux Normanñoz Wills Li Valiðoium
Rex est Anglozu bello conquestor ccoz

ɑ Wills Conquestor Anglie genuit de Alienora Regina

Robtin
Curte
hose

Wittin
Ruffu

henric
Regem

Adam
Comitissa
Bleseñt

Thebaldi
Comitis
Blesene

nuꝛaliꝛ

Consta
nria Comi
tissa Bri
tannie

ꝛaꝛe

Stepha
nii
Regis

Conquestor Regnauit xx annis xi mensiꝰ Cadamo iacet

THE NORMANS

1066-1154

WILLIAM I 1066-87
WILLIAM II 1087-1100
HENRY I 1100-35
STEPHEN 1135-54

Opposite: A fourteenth-century genealogical tree of
William the Conqueror and his Norman successors.

THE NORMANS AND ANGEVINS

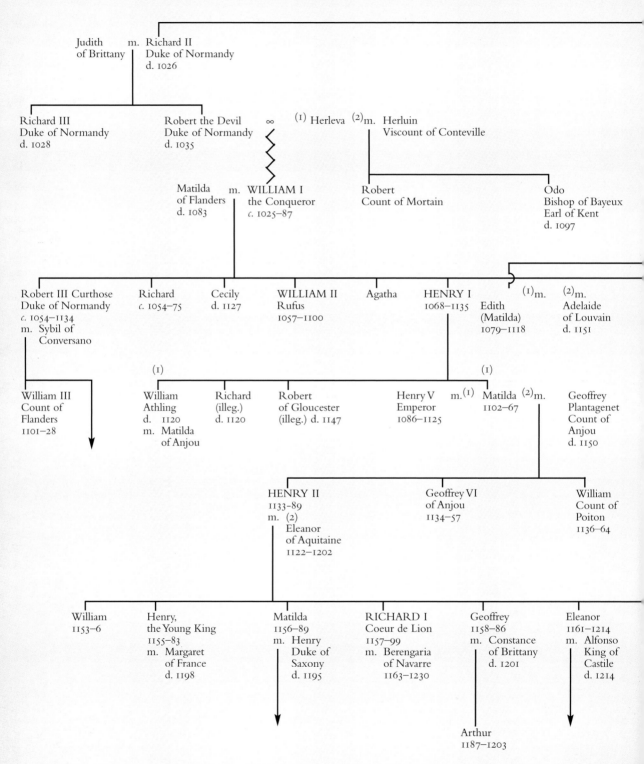

Judith of Brittany — m. Richard II Duke of Normandy d. 1026

Richard III Duke of Normandy d. 1028

Robert the Devil Duke of Normandy d. 1035 ∞ (1) Herleva (2)m. Herluin Viscount of Conteville

Robert Count of Mortain

Odo Bishop of Bayeux Earl of Kent d. 1097

Matilda of Flanders d. 1083 m. WILLIAM I the Conqueror *c.* 1025–87

Robert III Curthose Duke of Normandy *c.* 1054–1134 m. Sybil of Conversano

Richard *c.* 1054–75

Cecily d. 1127

WILLIAM II Rufus 1057–1100

Agatha

HENRY I 1068–1135

(1)m. Edith (Matilda) 1079–1118

(2)m. Adelaide of Louvain d. 1151

William III Count of Flanders 1101–28

(1) William Athling d. 1120 m. Matilda of Anjou

Richard (illeg.) d. 1120

Robert of Gloucester (illeg.) d. 1147

Henry V Emperor 1086–1125 m.(1)

(1) Matilda 1102–67 (2)m. Geoffrey Plantagenet Count of Anjou d. 1150

HENRY II 1133–89 m. (2) Eleanor of Aquitaine 1122–1202

Geoffrey VI of Anjou 1134–57

William Count of Poiton 1136–64

William 1153–6

Henry, the Young King 1155–83 m. Margaret of France d. 1198

Matilda 1156–89 m. Henry Duke of Saxony d. 1195

RICHARD I Coeur de Lion 1157–99 m. Berengaria of Navarre 1163–1230

Geoffrey 1158–86 m. Constance of Brittany d. 1201

Eleanor 1161–1214 m. Alfonso King of Castile d. 1214

Arthur 1187–1203

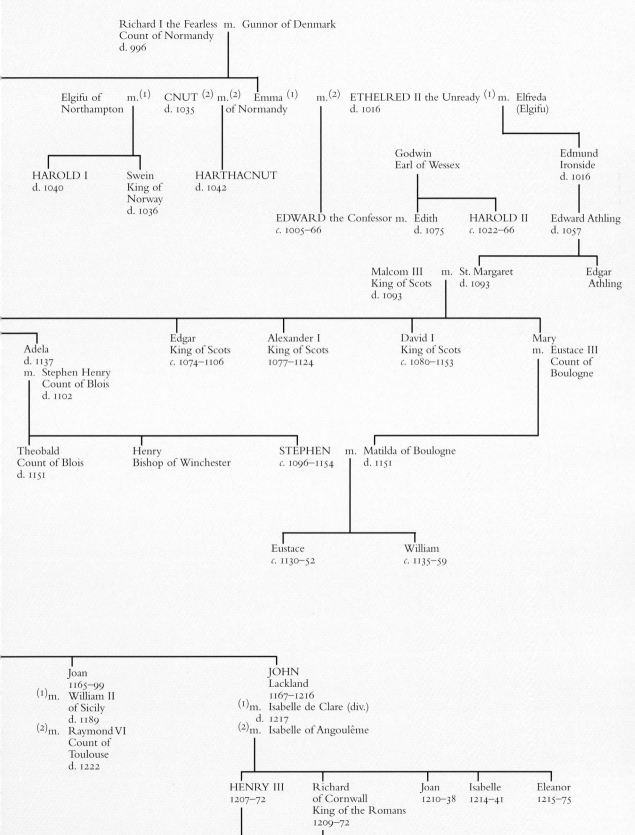

Richard I the Fearless m. Gunnor of Denmark
Count of Normandy
d. 996

Elgifu of   m.(1)   CNUT (2) m.(2) Emma (1)   m.(2)   ETHELRED II the Unready (1) m. Elfreda
Northampton   d. 1035   of Normandy   d. 1016   (Elgifu)

HAROLD I   Swein   HARTHACNUT   Godwin   Edmund
d. 1040   King of   d. 1042   Earl of Wessex   Ironside
                Norway   d. 1016
                d. 1036

                                        EDWARD the Confessor m. Edith   HAROLD II   Edward Athling
                                        c. 1005–66   d. 1075   c. 1022–66   d. 1057

                                                     Malcom III   m. St. Margaret   Edgar
                                                     King of Scots   d. 1093   Athling
                                                     d. 1093

Adela   Edgar   Alexander I   David I   Mary
d. 1137   King of Scots   King of Scots   King of Scots   m. Eustace III
m. Stephen Henry   c. 1074–1106   1077–1124   c. 1080–1153   Count of
    Count of Blois   Boulogne
    d. 1102

Theobald   Henry   STEPHEN   m. Matilda of Boulogne
Count of Blois   Bishop of Winchester   c. 1096–1154   d. 1151
d. 1151

                               Eustace   William
                               c. 1130–52   c. 1135–59

        Joan   JOHN
        1165–99   Lackland
(1)m.   William II   1167–1216
        of Sicily   (1)m. Isabelle de Clare (div.)
        d. 1189   d. 1217
(2)m.   Raymond VI   (2)m. Isabelle of Angoulême
        Count of
        Toulouse
        d. 1222

                      HENRY III   Richard   Joan   Isabelle   Eleanor
                      1207–72   of Cornwall   1210–38   1214–41   1215–75
                                       King of the Romans
                                       1209–72

WILLIAM I *r.* 1066-87

W ILLIAM WAS BORN AT ABOUT the time that his father, Robert, became Duke of Normandy (1028). William's mother was Herleva, daughter of a wealthy citizen of Falaise. Not long after William was born she was given in marriage to one of Duke Robert's followers and by him she had two more sons: Robert, who became Count of Mortain, and Odo, who was made Bishop of Bayeux in 1049 when he was not yet twenty years old. William therefore was illegitimate and most contemporary writers refer to him as William the Bastard. But he was his father's only son and shortly before Duke Robert went on a pilgrimage to Jerusalem (1034), he persuaded the Norman barons to recognise William as his heir. On the way home Robert died in Asia Minor and so, in 1035, young William found himself Duke of Normandy.

In practice this meant that for the next ten years Normandy was without a ruler and a great deal of disorder went unchecked. William was lucky to survive these years. Several of his cousins would have preferred to see him out of the way. He had some narrow escapes, but survive he did - largely thanks to the support of his mother's kinsmen. William's boyhood was spent among scenes of violence and intrigue. As a result he learned that not many men could be trusted, and those few in whom he did place his trust were mostly the friends he made in childhood.

In the mid-1040s William began to govern for himself. He was almost continuously at war, either against Norman rebels or neighbouring princes, or both. He became a hard and ruthless campaigner - though flatterers liked to say that he was the best knight in the world. His most powerful neighbours were King Henry of France, Count Geoffrey of Anjou and Count Baldwin of Flanders. Between 1052 and

Opposite: Manuscript page depicting Norman warriors at sea in readiness for battle.

Pages from the Domesday Book, a list of every major landowner and their sources of revenue that was compiled by commissioners, who started work in 1086 on William's orders. He had this enormous task undertaken to enable him to assess the wealth of the kingdom that he had conquered as he needed to know what resources were available to him.

1060 two of these, France and Anjou, were hostile to Normandy so it was well for William that he could count on the friendship of Flanders. He had asked Count Baldwin for the hand of his daughter Matilda, but in 1049 the Pope forbade the marriage, presumably on the grounds that William and Matilda were too closely related. Despite this William went ahead; the Flemish alliance was more important than papal disapproval. William and Matilda must have been an odd-looking couple. The evidence of the bones found in their graves suggests that he was about five foot ten inches tall and she about four foot two inches. But by all accounts it was a successful marriage. She bore at least nine children (four of them sons) and most contemporaries believed that William was never unfaithful to her.

In 1060 both King Henry and Count Geoffrey died. The heir to France was a small boy and in Anjou there was all the trouble of a dis-

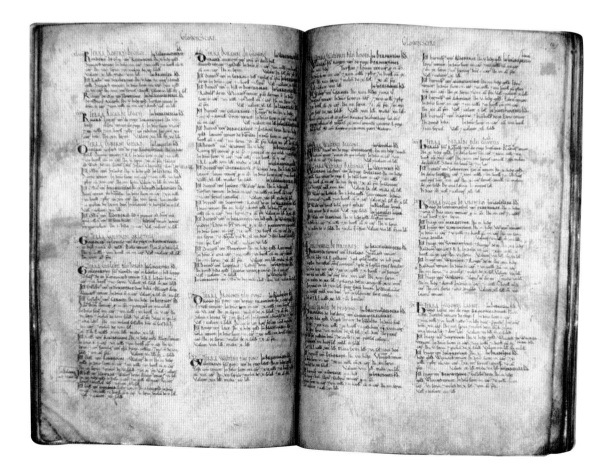

puted succession. The consequent weakness of his neighbours left the way clear for William to conquer the county of Maine in 1063 and then turn his eyes on England.

Although William was only a distant cousin of Edward the Confessor, in 1051, perhaps to win Norman support in a quarrel with his powerful father-in-law, Earl Godwin, Edward dangled before William the prospect of succeeding to the English throne. Edward himself was childless and since monarchs were not yet chosen in strict order of heredity, there were several candidates for the succession. Among these was Harold, son of Earl Godwin and brother of Edward's wife Edith. By 1066 Edward was reconciled with the Godwin family, and on his deathbed he nominated Harold, the chief magnate of the kingdom, as his heir.

William felt cheated and prepared at once for an invasion of England. He insisted that Edward had promised him the throne and that, on a visit to Normandy in 1064, Harold had sworn an oath to support his accession; he claimed that Harold was thus both usurper and perjurer and so won papal approval for his expedition. In the careful preparations for invasion William showed himself at his best. It was an enterprise far beyond the resources of his duchy and so he recruited soldiers from all over northern France and Flanders. The prospect of laying hands on the wealth of England, its land and its silver, attracted thousands to his banner. Throughout the spring and summer of 1066 ships were built and military supplies assembled. But however meticulous his preparations, William cannot have expected anything like the rapid and overwhelming success he in fact achieved. It must have seemed likely that he was facing many years of hard campaigning against an enemy whose wealth and military resources were greater than his own. But an extraordinary series of lucky chances brought things to a swift and dramatic conclusion.

By August 1066 William's expeditionary force was ready. If he had sailed when he wanted to he would have found Harold and an English fleet waiting to receive him. If he had managed to defeat the English he would then have had to face another contender for the throne, Harold Hardrada, the King of Norway and a famous Viking warrior. But, as it happened, throughout August and most of September the wind was against William. Merely to hold his waiting army together was, in these circumstances, a great achievement, yet while he impatiently kicked his heels some of his greatest problems were being solved for him. In September Harold Hardrada, accompanied by one of his wives and several of his children, reached the Tyne and then defeated the northern levies in a pitched battle near York. As soon as he heard of the Viking landing Harold Godwinsson marched north and routed Hardrada and his allies at Stamford Bridge on 25 September 1066. Two days later the wind in the Channel changed direction. William set sail and was able to make an unopposed landing at Pevensey. During the next two weeks his soldiers fortified their beachhead and pillaged the area. But what then? Would William dare march far inland, losing contact with his fleet and the line of communication with Normandy? Fortunately the problem was solved by Harold who came rushing back from the north and allowed William to challenge him to battle. If Harold had held aloof it is hard to see what William could have done, but Harold was confident of his military prowess and, as a new king with an uncertain title, he wished to see the matter settled once and for all. Thus on 14 October 1066 the two armies met at Hastings.

After a long and desperately hard struggle William's skilful handling of a combined force of archers and cavalry enabled him to break down the English shield wall. The fact that Harold and his brothers died fighting meant that after Hastings there was no leader capable of organising further resistance. The English earls and bishops hesitated, took a few indecisive steps and then decided to submit. On Christmas Day 1066 William was crowned in Westminster Abbey. In February 1067 he returned to Normandy leaving his half-brother Odo of Bayeux, now Earl of Kent, in charge. Apart from the destruction of the Godwinsson dynasty he left the English scene much as he had found it. All this, however, was to change as a result of the events of the next four years. All over England revolts broke out. They were unplanned and unco-ordinated. Some of the leaders, like Hereward the Wake, passed into legend, but none of them was capable of more than local action. Thus William was able to deal with one minor uprising after another and by 1071 he had subdued the whole country. The turbulent north had been devastated. Several hundred castles had been built and within their walls the outnumbered Normans could sleep safely. William punished rebels by confiscating their estates and giving them to Normans. Thus the native English aristocracy was wiped out. Within the areas covered by the Domesday Book only two English landowners of any note survived the Norman flood.

The English Church suffered the same fate as the English nobility. At William's request papal legates deposed five English bishops in 1070.

Illuminated manuscript of William, bearing the royal arms, riding with his soldiers. From the *Liber Legum Antiquorum Regum*, c. 1321.

They were replaced by men from the continent. Outstanding among them was Lanfranc, the new Archbishop of Canterbury. From now on whenever a bishop or an abbot died the same policy was pursued. By 1096 there was not a single bishopric or important abbey in English hands. The traditional learning and liturgy of the English Church was treated with contempt by men educated in the schools of Europe. Probably no other conquest in European history ever had such disastrous consequences for the defeated ruling class. This had not been intended, for William was a conservative by temperament; but he was also ruthless and when events pushed him to destroy then he destroyed thoroughly. His own prestige and power were of course tremendously enhanced. He was able to bestow huge gifts of land upon his followers without impoverishing himself. As for England, that was now ruled by a French-speaking aristocracy and although the broad outline of the social structure remained unchanged, there was an entirely new and alien ruling class; the language barrier only served to widen the gulf between it and the peasantry.

After 1071 William's hold on England was fairly secure and he came to regard it chiefly as a source of revenue. The extensive royal estates and the sophisticated English financial machinery brought in huge sums. The Welsh and the Scots gave him little trouble; Scandinavian rulers continued to look greedily towards England but the ever-present threat of another Viking invasion never quite materialised. From 1071 to 1084 most of William's attention was taken up by war and diplomacy on the continent. Normandy was his homeland and far more vulnerable to sudden attack than was his island kingdom. Moreover the King of France and the Counts of Anjou and Flanders were alarmed by William's newly acquired power and took every opportunity to diminish it. Their best opportunities were provided by William's eldest son Robert (born 1054). Recognised as the heir to Normandy as long ago as 1066 he had never been permitted to enjoy either money or power and from 1078 onwards he became involved in a series of intrigues, a tool in the hands of William's enemies. In one skirmish William was actually wounded by his son.

Then in 1085 William returned to England with a huge army of mercenaries ready to counter the invasion planned by King Swein of Denmark. The administrative effort involved in catering for this army seems to have persuaded William that he ought to have more precise information about the distribution of wealth among his barons. So in

1086 commissioners were sent from shire to shire and the results of their inquiries are now enshrined in the Domesday Book. It listed the major landholders in each county and provided William with a remarkably full description of their sources of revenue. But although the book has been of great value to historians, it seems unlikely that William was able to make much use of it. Before the end of the year he had been recalled to Normandy. Once again he found himself campaigning against the King of France and, as usual, the war was concentrated in the Vexin, a disputed territory lying between Rouen and Paris. In July 1087 William launched a surprise attack on Mantes and took it, but during the sack of the town he received the injury from which, on 9 September, he died. His body was carried to the church of St Stephen at Caen for burial.

Unfortunately during the last few years William had grown very fat. King Philip of France used to say that he looked like a pregnant woman. When the attendants tried to force his body into the stone sarcophagus it burst and filled the church with a foul smell. It was an unpleasant ending, but unlike many kings he had unquestionably lived more successfully than he died. Few kings can have enjoyed so much luck as William the Bastard, but few took such full advantage of their good fortune as William the Conqueror, founder of a new royal dynasty.

WILLIAM II *r.* 1087–1100

ILLIAM, THE THIRD SON OF William of Normandy and Matilda, was born about 1057. Almost nothing is known of his youth, but it is at least clear that the time he spent in the household of Archbishop Lanfranc made little impression upon him. He was deeply attached to his father and while Robert rebelled, William never wavered in his loyalty. When Richard, the second son, died in a hunting accident in the New Forest it seemed possible that William might take Robert's place as chief heir. William, moreover, was at the bedside of the dying King to hear his last wishes while Robert remained at the court of his father's enemy, Philip of France. But the custom which gave the ancestral lands, the patrimony, to the first-born son proved too strong. Robert succeeded to Normandy. To William, however, the old King gave his newly conquered land, England. Following the instructions of the old King's will, Lanfranc crowned William at Westminster on 26 September 1087. Like his father, William was inclined to stoutness. He had fair hair, piercing eyes, a red face (thus his nickname Rufus) and a tendency to stutter when excited.

The division of the Conqueror's lands created political difficulties. Many Norman lords held estates on both sides of the Channel. Their dilemma was summed up by the greatest of them, the new King's uncle, Odo of Bayeux. 'How can we give proper service to two mutually hostile and distant lords? If we serve Duke Robert well we shall offend his brother William, and he will deprive us of our revenues and honours in England. On the other hand if we obey King William, Duke Robert will deprive us of our patrimonies in Normandy.' By 1088 it was already plain that some barons, inspired by Odo, would prefer to have Robert as their lord on both sides of the sea. But

Opposite: Pope Urban II preaches the First Crusade at the Council of Clermont in 1095. In order to join the crusade William I's eldest son Robert pawned Normandy to his brother William II.

Robert failed to appear in England, William acted firmly and the revolt soon collapsed. Now it was the younger brother's turn. In 1089 he laid claim to Normandy. With English silver he was able to buy support in Normandy. Gradually Robert's position became more and more difficult until in 1096 he was glad to join the crusade preached by Pope Urban II. In order to equip himself and his retinue for the long march he pawned Normandy to William for 10,000 marks.

The new Duke's main task was to recover Maine and the Vexin, lost during Robert's slack rule. By 1099 he had successfully accomplished this. In England meanwhile he had, in 1095, suppressed a rebellion led by Robert Mowbray, Earl of Northumberland. In Wales and Scotland the Normans were on the march again. On every front William's combination of diplomacy, bribery and war proved effective; an archbishop of Lyons referred to him as 'the victorious King of the English'.

Yet for all his success as a generous leader of soldiers William's reputation has remained consistently low. Unfortunately for him the history of the time was written almost entirely by monks and they did not like him; nor did he respect them. On one occasion when a monk came to him to report a dream in which he had foreseen William's death, the King dismissed him mockingly – 'he is a monk and so, of course, he dreams for money'. After the death of Lanfranc in 1089 Rufus seemed to throw off all restraints. Serious-minded churchmen, accustomed to the conventional piety and sober discretion of his father's court, were appalled by the gaiety and licentiousness which prevailed under his son. Since neither mistresses nor illegitimate children are ever mentioned in connection with William it is possible that he was a homosexual. He never married. He was sceptical of religion's claims and treated the Church purely as a rich corporation which needed taxing. He was never in a hurry to appoint bishops and abbots, for during vacancies he could help himself to the Church's revenues. In carrying out these profitable policies Rufus relied on the ingenious aid of the quick-witted and worldly clerk Ranulf Flambard, whom he eventually made Bishop of Durham.

Above all, William's reputation has suffered because in 1093 when he thought he was dying he appointed a saint as Archbishop of Canterbury (after keeping the see vacant for four years). What made this appointment so disastrous from William's point of view was the fact that it occurred at a time when a European movement for Church reform was creating an atmosphere in which saints were only too likely to become political radicals. The new Archbishop was Anselm, a scholar monk who had previously been Abbot of Bec. As a Norman abbot Anselm had already sworn to obey Urban II; but in England neither Urban II nor his rival Clement III were recognised as Pope. William, following in his father's footsteps, preferred to remain uncommitted and he was angry when Anselm took it for granted that Urban was the rightful Pope. In 1095 the King called a council at Rockingham in order to settle this and other matters which were in dispute between him and Anselm. But to the consternation of all, Anselm appealed to Rome, claiming that as Archbishop of Canterbury he could not be judged in a secular court. This was too much for Rufus who now determined to rid himself of the Archbishop. He would even recognise Urban if the Pope, in his turn, would depose Anselm. A papal legate was sent to England and Urban was publicly proclaimed as the canonical Pope; but this achieved, the legate would make no move against Anselm. Dismayed by the failure of his plot William continued to harass the Archbishop and he never showed any sympathy for his attempts to reform the Church. Eventually Anselm could bear it no longer. In 1097 he sailed from Dover, leaving the Canterbury estates to be taken into the King's hands.

Besides helping to blacken William's reputation, the quarrel with Anselm is a significant indication of the growing importance of the papacy. For centuries no one had taken much notice of the bishops of Rome but now, as a result of the eleventh-century Gregorian reform movement (named after its most zealous advocate, Pope Gregory VII), they began to wield an influence which not even Rufus could entirely ignore. In the short run, however, William II had gained from the quarrel. In 1100 he enjoyed the revenues of three bishoprics and twelve abbeys. Nor was there as yet any sign that the conflict had tarnished men's belief in the potency of royal magic. Even Eadmer, the Canterbury monk who wrote the *Life of Anselm*, noted that 'the wind and the sea seemed to obey him. Whenever he wished to cross from England to Normandy or back again every storm – and sometimes the storm was raging wildly – was stilled so that his crossings were always attended by a wonderful calm.' Indeed, Eadmer went on, 'in war and in the acquisition of territory he enjoyed such success that you would think the whole world smiling upon him.'

But on 2 August 1100, at the height of his success and full of plans for further conquests, William was struck down by an arrow while out hunting in the New Forest. It may have been an accident, or murder. His body was carried to Winchester and interred in the cathedral directly below the main tower. In the following year the tower collapsed – though, as one monk wrote, 'it might have collapsed anyway, even if he had not been buried there'.

HENRY I *r.* 1100-35

ENRY, THE FOURTH SON OF William and Matilda, was born in England in 1068. He was better educated than his brothers and felt at ease in the company of learned men. From this time onwards the Kings of England were normally able to read. From his dying father he received no land, but was given instead £5,000 in silver – an enormous sum. At once he left the old King's bedside and hurried to the Treasury to supervise the weighing out of the money. When his elder brothers, Robert of Normandy and William of England, quarrelled, he flitted from side to side, always seeking his own advantage and eventually making himself thoroughly distrusted by both. In 1091 they were temporarily reconciled and marched together against Henry. They made a treaty whereby they agreed that if either died without leaving a legitimate son he would be succeeded by the other. This agreement was to disinherit Henry.

When Robert went on crusade Henry's hopes naturally rose. Should the childless William die now, he was the man on the spot and the obvious heir. But by the summer of 1100 everyone knew that Robert was on his way home, accompanied by a rich and beautiful wife and basking in the prestige due to a man who had fought his way into Jerusalem. Henry's chance seemed to be slipping away from him. Perhaps it was just coincidence that William died when he did and where he did – for Henry too was hunting in the New Forest on 2 August 1100. As soon as he knew that his brother was dead Henry moved fast; it was as though he had been prepared for it. He rode to Winchester and took possession of the Treasury. From there he went straight to Westminster where he was crowned on 5 August. On the same day he issued his coro-

Opposite: An illuminated manuscript page showing the king, top right, sitting on his throne. The French fleur du lys have been incorporated into the background, to the left of the king. Below him is the *White Ship* in some distress; it foundered and Prince William, the heir to the throne, was drowned, throwing the king's dynastic ambitions into disarray.

cui successit Henricus frater
eius z regnauit annis xxxvi.
hic erat pastor ferax z custos
nemoz suit z sapiens z stre
nuuus dux noemannie que
auersinus ambrosius Leonem iusticie
in historia Begum noiauit ffecit qz em
iusticium z iusticiam in terra dixit qz
uxorem generosam z optimam de
nobili genere anglorz. z diuonu p
quam multum sibi confederauit Reg
num scilicet asiam pncipis sui Alba
nie uita z moribz oznatam sororem
scilicet Alexandri pncipis sui scocie
z dauidis scocie qui postea suit pnceps
Albanie. Cui uero Rex Henricus psa
tus dedit honorem de huntingdon
cum matilda cognate sua que erat
uxor puus pmi simonis de scenlis
comitis de huntingdon z worshmp
ton cum custodia puerorum suorz et die
concordes ad muicem semder effecti
suerunt quia predtus Alexander ven
sicatur sibi iure hereditario cozona
z monarchiam tocius Begum preda
sicut uerus heres z iustus de iure boni
Regis Echardi ultimi. Alexte qz diu
cuiz omnia dictauit qz diam etiam in
multis p locis ffecit qz bonu in gentu
totum malum qz deleuit uocabatur
matild z Begina optima. Obiit uo
predictus Henricus in noemannia
apud z yrouns. sepultus enim suit
in anglia apud Redinges in Alba
thia quam construxerat. matilda
uero Begina predicta sepulta suit
in anglia apud Westmonasteruii
cuius anime spicietur deus.

¶ henricus primus genuit

Willm
qui periit
in mari

Ricm
qui piit
in mari

matil
dam im
pteicē

Ricdi
q obiit

hennc
Regis se
cundi

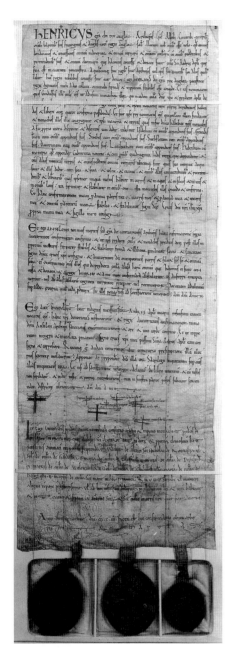

nation charter, renouncing the oppressive practices of his brother and promising good government.

A few weeks later Robert arrived back in Normandy. Henry had to prepare to meet the inevitable invasion. His policy was to buy support by granting favours and making wide-ranging concessions along the lines laid down in the coronation charter. 'If they ask for it give them York or even London' was the advice given to Henry by his shrewdest counsellor Count Robert of Meulan. By inviting Anselm to return to England he hoped to win over both the English church and the papacy; by marrying (in November 1100) Edith, sister of King Edgar of Scotland, he was ensuring that he would not be attacked in the north while he had his hands full in the south. He secured the alliance of France and Flanders, neither of whom wanted to see England and Normandy united under one all-too-powerful ruler. Thus when Robert landed at Portsmouth in July 1101 he found he could make little headway. With Anselm as the intermediary a treaty was arranged. Henry was to keep England and pay his brother an annual pension of £2,000.

But not for one moment did Henry trust those who had hoped to protect their Norman estates by aiding Duke Robert in 1101. Above all he distrusted the rich and brutal Earl of Shrewsbury, Robert of Bellême, and he set about the task of breaking him. This he accomplished in 1102. He captured Robert's chief strongholds in the Welsh Marches and then banished him. But Robert, like others in his position, found in his Norman properties a safe base from which he could hope to organised the recovery of his English lands. By perpetuating the division of the Conqueror's lands the treaty of 1101 had ensured the continuance of political instability. So the pattern of the previous reign was repeated as Henry gradually manoeuvred himself into a commanding position in Normandy. In 1106 the issue was decided by the battle of Tinchebrai. The knights in Henry's vanguard dismounted in order to beat off the charge of Duke Robert's cavalry. Robert himself was captured in the battle and spent the last twenty-eight years of his life as his brother's prisoner. Other great barons who fell into Henry's hands, including Robert of Bellême, were also condemned to life imprisonment.

Although in the first years of his reign Henry was preoccupied with Norman affairs, he was not as free to concentrate on them as he would have liked. Traditional royal rights over the church were threatened by the new ideas associated with the Gregorian reform movement. The reformers did not only wish to purify the moral and spiritual life of the clergy; in order to do so they believed that it was necessary to free the church from secular control. The most hated symbol of this control was lay investiture, a ceremony in which a new abbot or bishop received the ring and staff of office from the hands of the secular prince who had appointed him. Although the first papal decree against lay investiture had been issued as long ago as 1059 and many more prohibitions had been published since, no one in England seems to have been aware of their existence until Anselm returned in the autumn of 1100. While in exile he had attended papal councils at Bari (1098) and Rome (1099). There he learned of the papal attitude to lay investiture. Thus although he himself had been invested by Rufus in 1093 he now refused either to do homage to Henry or to consecrate those prelates whom Henry had invested. This placed the King in a difficult position. Bishops and abbots were great landowners and key figures in central and local administration; he needed their assistance and had to be sure of their loyalty. On the other hand, unlike Rufus, he was unwilling to provoke a quarrel, so for years he found it more convenient to postpone the problem rather than try to solve it. Henry's delaying tactics were intolerable to Anselm and in 1103 he once again took the path into exile.

But then, in 1105, at a critical moment in Henry's Normandy campaign, the Pope threatened to excommunicate him so the King hastened to come to terms. Agreement was reached in 1106 and ratified at a council in London in 1107. Henry renounced lay investiture, but prelates were to continue to do homage for their fiefs. In practice the King's wishes continued to be the decisive factor in the making of bishops. To some extent it can be said that Henry gave up the form but preserved the reality of control. When Anselm died in 1109 he kept the see of Canterbury vacant for five years. Yet he had lost something and he knew it. In the fierce war of propaganda which accompanied the 'Investiture Contest' the Gregorians had insisted that the King was a layman, nothing more, and as such he was inferior to all priests, for priests were concerned with the soul and the King only with the body. The Church

Opposite: In his coronation charter Henry I promised good government. From left to right the signatures are: Henry I, Archbishop Anselm, Gilbert, Lord of Tonbridge, Queen Matilda, the Bishop of Rochester, Count Robert of Meulan and Henry, Earl of Warenne.

could no longer tolerate the old idea that anointed kings were sacred deputies of God. In giving up lay investiture Henry was acknowledging the merely secular nature of his office. It was an important moment in the history of kingship. And yet it is precisely at this time that we first come across the claim that kings possessed a healing magic. It was said that if a person suffering from scrofula were touched by a king, the disease – known as the 'king's evil' – would at once be cleared up. Whatever learned churchmen might say, in popular thought there was still something miraculous in kingship.

Once Normandy had been conquered and a compromise solution found to the investiture dispute, Henry's main concern was to hold on to what he had. Few kings ever did this more tenaciously or effectively. He was a hard man who knew how to keep men loyal; he may not have won their hearts but they looked forward to the rewards he had to offer and they certainly feared his wrath. In 1090 he had pushed a man off the top of Rouen Castle for betraying the oath of allegiance which he had sworn to Duke Robert. With this example before them men took seriously the oaths which they swore to King Henry. The most famous of the King's servants was Roger of Salisbury, the archetypal bureaucrat, competent and discreet. Under his direction there are clear signs of the development of the English civil service, notably the rise of the court of the Exchequer.

Normandy, of course, was the most vulnerable part of his empire and after 1106 Henry spent more than half the remainder of his reign there facing the traditional enemies of the Norman dukes. The year 1118, as described by the Anglo-Saxon Chronicle, was typical. 'King Henry spent the whole of this year in Normandy on account of the war with the King of France, Count of Anjou and Count of Flanders … England paid dearly for all this in numerous taxes from which there was no relief all year.' By 1119 all seemed well. Henry, who never risked battle until he had already won the diplomatic war which preceded it, beat King Louis VI of France in the battle of Brémule. Angevin friendship had been secured by the marriage of his only legitimate son, William, to the daughter of the Count of Anjou. But the whole carefully contrived edifice came tumbling down when William was drowned in the wreck of the *White Ship* (November 1120).

From then on the succession problem dominated the politics of the reign. Less than three months after William's death Henry married Adelaide of Louvain (his first wife, Edith, had died in 1118), but the hoped-for heir was never born. So although Henry acknowledged more than twenty bastards he was survived by only one legitimate child, his daughter Matilda. When her husband, the Emperor Henry V of Germany, died in 1125 Henry recalled her to his court and made the barons swear to accept her as their ruler in the event of his dying without a male heir. Somewhat against her will Matilda was then in 1128 married to a sixteen-year-old boy, Geoffrey of Anjou, for Henry was determined to continue the Angevin alliance. But the prospect of being ruled by an Angevin did not please the Norman barons and Geoffrey was well aware of this fact. Thus he asked to be given custody of some key Norman castles while Henry was still alive and able to help. But the old King refused to give up any of his power. The result, in summer 1135, was war. In these melancholy circumstances Henry died, supposedly of a surfeit of lampreys, in December 1135.

Although he ruled for thirty-five years few English kings are as little known as Henry I. Careful, sober, harsh and methodical he chose his servants from men of a similar stamp. When compared with Rufus and Ranulf Flambard, Henry I and Roger of Salisbury are drab and colour-less characters. But from 1102 until the end of his reign there was no revolt in England. A king who could keep the peace for over thirty years was a master of the art of government.

STEPHEN *r.* 1135-54

STEPHEN WAS A YOUNGER SON of the Count of Blois and Champagne, also Stephen, and of Adela, daughter of William the Conqueror. He was born about 1096, some half-dozen years earlier than his cousin and rival for the Crown, Henry 1's daughter Matilda. Stephen's mother was a formidable woman. When her husband returned early from the First Crusade she sent him away again. As a result he was killed in the Holy Land in 1102 and responsibility for seeing that young Stephen was properly looked after fell upon his uncle the King of England. King Henry provided for him on a grand scale. He granted him estates on both sides of the Channel and by 1130 Stephen was the richest man in his uncle's empire. Henry 1 also looked after Stephen's younger brother, Henry of Blois, making him both Abbot of Glastonbury and Bishop of Winchester, and thus the wealthiest churchman in England. By his generosity Henry made sure that Stephen's elder brother, Count Theobald of Blois, did not join the Norman coalition organised by France and Anjou. In 1125 Stephen married Matilda, the heiress to the county of Boulogne. Her loyalty and energy were to be a great help to Stephen in later years and meanwhile the acquisition of her territories, which included the port of Wissant, meant that Stephen was profitably placed to dominate cross-Channel trade.

Inevitably Henry 1's death in 1135 was followed by a dispute over the succession. There were very few Anglo-Norman lords who wished to be ruled by his daughter and her Angevin husband. One group of Norman barons wanted to elect Count Theobald of Blois but their deliberations were cut short by the news that Theobald's younger brother Stephen had already been crowned (22 December 1135).

Illuminated manuscript showing King Stephen, with a hawk and prey, sitting on his throne. He managed to keep hold of the English throne, but the death of his son Eustace meant that it eventually fell in Angevin hands.

Advised by Henry of Blois and acting with great decisiveness Stephen had crossed the Channel and taken control of England. Count Theobald at once dropped his claim to the crown, but he still hoped to become Duke of Normandy. The Norman lords, however, were not prepared to face again the problem of divided loyalties; to Theobald's disappointment they transferred their allegiance to Stephen.

For two years Stephen had little trouble, but in 1138 Geoffrey of Anjou invaded Normandy, King David of Scotland (Matilda's uncle) invaded the north, and Robert of Gloucester (Matilda's half-brother) raised the standard of rebellion in the west country. Initially Stephen was able to weather the storm, but he then made three fatal mistakes. In December 1138 he offended Henry of Blois by not making him

Archbishop of Canterbury. In the summer of 1139 he arrested three influential 'civil-service' bishops, including the great Roger of Salisbury, and thus enabled Henry of Blois to claim that ecclesiastical liberties had been infringed. In the autumn, when Matilda fell into his hands, he allowed her to go free when the ruthless, if unchivalrous, thing to do was to keep her in prison. From now on there were always two rival courts in England, though Stephen was generally in a better position than the Empress, who rarely held more than a few west country shires. Their relative strengths are indicated by the number of surviving charters: 720 issued by Stephen, only 88 by Matilda. But at one stage Matilda had a clear-cut chance of victory. In February 1141 Stephen rashly accepted battle at Lincoln and fought on bravely when he might have escaped. As a result he was captured and put in prison in Bristol. Henry of Blois, now acting as papal legate, openly went over to the Empress's side and in the summer she was able to enter London. But she spurned the peace terms worked out by the legate and offended the Londoners with her high-handed and tactless behaviour. When Stephen's Queen, Matilda of Boulogne, advanced towards the city the Londoners took up arms and drove the Empress out. Thus the planned coronation at Westminster never took place, and Matilda never became Queen of England. A few months later Robert of Gloucester was captured and as he was the mainstay of her party Matilda had to agree to an exchange of prisoners: Stephen for Robert. Her chance of winning the crown was lost and the status quo in England was restored.

In 1142 Robert left England on a mission to Geoffrey of Anjou. But Matilda's husband had his hands full in Normandy and Anjou and refused to disperse his forces still further. Taking full advantage of Robert's absence Stephen moved rapidly and after a skilful diversionary move laid siege to Oxford Castle where Matilda was in residence. This time he was determined not to let her go and pressed the siege relentlessly. But once again the Empress escaped. One December night she was lowered by rope from the castle walls, and with just four companions – all of them wrapped in white cloaks, for there was snow on the ground – she crossed the frozen river on foot, passed through the King's pickets and made her way to safety. After the violent see-saw of fortunes in 1141–2, the civil war settled down into a kind of routine. Stephen's habit of arresting without warning men who were supposed to be his supporters tended to lose him friends, but neither side could make much headway at a time when the art of war revolved around castles

and the defenders generally held the advantage. In October 1147 Robert of Gloucester died. Disheartened, the Empress left England early in 1148, never to return. Next year the struggle was taken up by Matilda's son Henry fitzEmpress, but the sixteen-year-old youth simply did not have the resources to alter the balance of power, and while he remained in England, in danger of being captured, he put the whole Angevin cause in jeopardy. It was better that he should return to Normandy and consolidate his position there.

If Stephen ever felt confident that he was going to win the civil war then a glance at Normandy should have made him realise that he would not. The Normans had been thrown into confusion by the news of Stephen's capture at Lincoln and Geoffrey of Anjou had at once taken advantage of the situation. By the time of Stephen's release he had clearly gained the upper hand and few Normans were prepared to fight a losing war on behalf of a king who took so little interest in them – only once in his entire reign, in 1137, did he even visit Normandy. In 1144 Rouen fell and Geoffrey was solemnly proclaimed Duke. From now on those English barons who also held land in Normandy had

A fifteenth-century picture of Empress Matilda in the history of England written by the monks of St Albans. Though never able to realise her ambition of becoming Queen of England, through her marriage to Geoffrey Plantagenet, Duke of Anjou, she bore Henry II, founder of the royal Plantagenet dynasty.

good cause not to offend the Empress and her son. The result was a stalemate which Stephen was unable to break.

In the last years of his reign Stephen's chief ambition was to secure the throne for his elder son, Eustace. He planned to have him crowned King in his own lifetime and for this he required the co-operation of Theobald, Archbishop of Canterbury. But since 1148 the Archbishop had shown that he had a mind of his own, and although he was prepared to recognise Stephen as king he would do nothing which would tend to prolong the civil war. So, with papal backing, he refused to grant Stephen's request.

In January 1153 Henry fitzEmpress returned to England. He was now a great man: lord of Anjou and Normandy and, in the right of his wife,

Eleanor, ruler of Aquitaine. By now it was generally accepted that peace would come only if Henry was recognised as Stephen's heir. The baronial class as a whole was never in favour of long-drawn-out hostilities; their landed estates were too vulnerable to the ravages of war. The problem was to make Stephen see it in the same light. The task was made unexpectedly simple when Eustace died in August 1153. Stephen's second son, William, had never expected to be King and so the way was opened for a negotiated peace. By the Treaty of Westminster it was agreed that Stephen should hold the kingdom for his life and that he should adopt Henry as his son and heir. William was to inherit all Stephen's baronial lands. This, in essence, was a repeat of the peace terms proposed by Henry of Blois in 1141. Matilda's intransigence then had cost the country another twelve years of civil war. Now, at last, Stephen could rule unchallenged and at peace, but he was a tired man and he did not live long to enjoy it. On 25 October 1154 he died and was buried by the side of his wife and elder son in the monastery they had founded at Faversham.

It is clear that Stephen must take some responsibility for the troubles of his reign. It is true that he was faced by a disputed succession, but then so were William I, William II and Henry I. Stephen was a much more attractive character than any of these Kings, but he lacked their masterfulness. Without it he was unable to dominate either his court or his kingdom. Yet he was no fool and occasionally he made the mistake of trying to be too clever. But it was hard not to like Stephen. Even a chronicler who wrote under the patronage of Robert of Gloucester had to concede that 'by his good nature and by the way he jested and enjoyed himself even in the company of his inferiors, Stephen earned an affection that can hardly be imagined'. He was a competent commander and a gallant knight – too brave perhaps for his own good. Basically he was a kind and amiable man whose friends would not abandon him when he was in trouble.

Above all, of course, he owed much to the courage of his wife in the critical months after the battle of Lincoln. In sharp contrast, Matilda's marriage to Geoffrey of Anjou was an unhappy one, and in 1141 her tactlessness and arrogance provided an object lesson in how to lose friends. Thus Stephen was unlikely to lose the war, but lacked the qualities which were needed to win it. Yet he never lost heart, remaining cheerful and buoyant until the day when the sudden death of his son Eustace made the whole nineteen years seem pointless. Then he resigned himself to the inevitable.

SOME ATTRIBUTED ARMS OF PRE-NORMAN KINGS

THE FIRST ENGLISH KING TO bear truly heraldic arms was Richard I. This means that those who came before him, although they may have used various devices, cannot be regarded as having borne coat armour.

However, the ingenious heralds of the Middle Ages amused themselves by designing arms for the pre-armorial monarchs. As early as the mid-thirteenth century Matthew Paris illustrated his *Historia Anglorum* with arms both real and attributed. Not surprisingly, different heralds often made different attributions, so that one king may have had several coats attributed to him at various times and by various armorists, not necessarily professional heralds. The shields illustrated here are perhaps more frequently used than many, as they are taken from a comprehensive roll of attributed arms contained in an early seventeenth-century manuscript (L14) in the library of the College of Arms.

The first row of shields shows those assigned to Arthur, who probably flourished at the beginning of the sixth century, Alfred, King of Wessex (died *c.* 899) and his grandson Athelstan (died 940).

The first shield in the second row is that of Athelstan's half-brother Edmund 'The Elder', who was murdered in 946. The next is that of Edmund's brother Edred (died 955), and the last is that of his son Edwy 'The Fair', who succeeded his uncle and died in 959.

The third row contains the arms attributed to both Edgar 'The Peaceful' (Edwy's brother), who died in 975, and to his eldest son Edward 'The Martyr', who was murdered at Corfe Castle in 978. The shield in the middle is that of Ethelred 'The Unready', the martyr's half-brother, who was deposed in 1013 and died three years later. Edmund Ironside's is the last shield. He was Ethelred's son and died in 1016.

The throne was usurped by Cnut (died 1035) whose second wife Emma was Ethelred's widow and a great-aunt of William the Conqueror. His arms are the first in the bottom row. The centre shield is that of St Edward 'The Confessor' and the third is that of Harold II. Both kings died in 1066.

The arms attributed to St Edward were used by King Richard II out of devotion to the saint and have become universally accepted. The coat is based on the reverse of a penny minted in Edward's reign.

RP

THE ARMS OF
THE NORMAN KINGS

THE FIRST FIVE POST-CONQUEST kings witnessed the birth of heraldry and there is evidence to suggest that they favoured the use of a lion as a symbol.

The coat of two gold lions *passant guardant* on a red shield is frequently attributed to the early Norman kings, although Matthew Paris backdates the coat of three lions and makes it do for all the Norman kings including Stephen. Others attribute a quite different coat to Stephen, presumably because he was not of the House of Normandy, although Henry II, the first Angevin king, is accorded the lions. Stephen's arms are illustrated beside those of the Normans and consist of a gold sagittary on red. This coat is given in College of Arms manuscript L14 but a coat consisting of three sagittaries firing over their shoulders is also frequently used and is mentioned in a treatise on heraldry written by Nicholas Upton *c.* 1400.

Henry II's Queen, Eleanor of Aquitaine, lived until 1204 and the reverse of her seal, cut after her husband's death, shows a shield bearing the three lions. This coat later appears on the second great seal of Richard I and thereafter is universally recognised as the royal arms of England and was used by succeeding monarchs until, in about 1340, Edward III styled himself King of France and assumed the royal arms of France, quartering them with English arms.

The beasts in the arms of England are frequently referred to as leopards. This is not because they were ever shown as or regarded as leopards but because the early heralds described a lion when rampant (rearing up aggressively) as a *lion*, but when walking along, whether looking to his front or looking out of the shield, as a *leopard*, really a contraction for leopard-like lion. Later, to avoid confusion, this term was dropped in favour of *passant*. Later still refinements in the blazon of a lion *passant* were adopted, the simple term *passant* being used simply for a lion looking ahead. When he looked out of the shield, like a lion of England, he became *passant guardant* and when he was shown looking over his shoulder he was *passant reguardant*.

THE ANGEVINS
1154-1216

HENRY II 1154-89

RICHARD I 1189-99

JOHN 1199-1216

Opposite: From Matthew Paris's chronicles, the Angevin Kings of England
are represented as patrons of the church – each is holding a model of a
church he founded. Left to right, top row: Henry II and Richard I.
Bottom row, left: John.

HENRY II *r.* 1154-89

ENRY WAS BORN AT LE MANS on 4 March 1133. He was the first of three sons born to Matilda, daughter of Henry I, by her second husband Count Geoffrey of Anjou. He first came to England in 1142 in order to show the world that there was more to the Angevin cause than his mother's haughty behaviour. Having successfully carried out his first foray into the world of politics, the nine-year-old Henry returned to the greater security of his father's dominions. By the time he was fourteen he was eager to try his luck again and in 1147 he arrived in England with a small band of mercenaries. But he soon ran out of money. Both his mother and Robert of Gloucester disapproved of his escapade and refused to help. So with the impudence of youth he applied to the man against whom he was fighting and with characteristic generosity Stephen sent him enough money to pay off his mercenaries and go home. Two years later Henry was back. First he went north to be knighted by his great-uncle, King David of Scotland. But their military plans went awry and Henry only just managed to avoid being captured in one of the ambushes laid for him. Yet his early life was not all adventure. His education was in the hands of famous scholars and he grew up with a love of reading and a taste for intellectual discussion.

Soon he was Lord of Normandy (from January 1150) and Anjou (at his father's death in September 1151). In May 1152 he married Eleanor of Aquitaine, the greatest heiress in Western Europe, just eight weeks after her marriage to King Louis VII of France had been annulled, ostensibly on grounds of consanguinity but in reality because in fourteen years of marriage she had failed to bear him a son. Henry and Eleanor had better luck. In the first six years of their marriage she had five chil-

Opposite: The great seal of Henry II. The king is shown sitting on his throne holding a sword and an orb, ancient symbols of kingship. His accession to the throne was the first uncontested change of monarch in England since the Conquest.

H. Rex Angl. ⁊ Dux Norm. ⁊ Aquit. ⁊ Com. And. Epo Exoniensi ⁊ Vic. ⁊ Prepositis ⁊ Ministr Exon.
⁊ Omnib; Baronib; ⁊ fidelib; suis Deuenesire. ⁊ Omnib; burgensib; Exon. Sat. Sciatis me concessisse ⁊
firmasse Ecclie Scē Trinitat de Lond. ⁊ Canonicis ibidem do samulantib; in ppetuū p anima
H. Reg. dni mei ⁊ Regine Matild auie mee ⁊ Mea. xxv. lib. ad Scalam p annū. de Redditib;
Ciuitatis Exon. qs Rex H. ⁊ Predicta Regina Matild. eis in elemosinā ppetuā dedint. Quare uolo
⁊ firmit Precipio. qd Vic quicūq; sit et fuerit in Exon. eas reddat pfatis Canonicis singlis annis
sic unq melius ⁊ plenius reddite fuerit. Et eisdē Terminis quib; reddi solebant. T. Alien. Regina ⁊ Her
to Albrinc Epo. ⁊ Tom Cancell. ⁊ Ric de Luci. ⁊ Vmfr de bohon. Dap. ⁊ Rad de hast. Ap Lond.

dren, four of them boys: William, who died very young, Henry, Richard and Geoffrey. Altogether they had eight children, the last of whom, John, was born in 1167. Eleanor was a remarkable woman, surrounded all her life by an aura of romance and scandalous rumour. A German poet wrote:

> Were the world all mine
> From the sea to the Rhine
> I'd give all away
> If the English Queen
> Would be mine for a day.

None the less after 1167 she and Henry drifted apart and towards the end of the reign she spent the greater part of each year in prison while he enjoyed a succession of mistresses.

In January 1153 Henry surprised Stephen by crossing the Channel in midwinter. By this time the English magnates were weary of war and convinced that peace would come only if Stephen recognised the justice of the Angevin claim. Under pressure from their supporters the two leaders made a series of truces which were turned into a permanent peace when the death of his son Eustace persuaded Stephen to give up the struggle. By the Treaty of Westminster (Christmas 1153) he was allowed to keep the kingdom on condition that he adopt Henry as his son and heir. Thus when Stephen died in October 1154 Henry took over without difficulty; it was the first undisputed succession to the throne since the Conquest. Henry was now the greatest prince in Western Europe, lord of an empire which stretched from the Scottish border to the Pyrenees. But it is important to remember that although England provided him with great wealth as well as a royal title, the heart of the empire lay elsewhere, in Anjou, the land of his fathers.

In England his first task was to destroy those baronial castles which had been built without royal licence and make good the losses suffered during Stephen's reign. By 1158 these two aims had been achieved. In addition the English King's overlordship of Scotland and Wales had been restored. But it was naturally his continental dominions which took up most of his attention. They were always more vulnerable than the island kingdom and more interesting too, since socially and culturally England was a bit of a backwater compared with France. Henry spent twenty-one of the thirty-four years of his reign on the continent. He began by re-

Opposite: Scenes from an illuminated manuscript showing the murder in 1180 of Thomas Becket in Canterbury Cathedral, an act which scandalised the Christian world and led to Becket's swift canonisation.

ef care; gentr apud dim amboſino.

x inſpato & in triſtia in
di gra pptiante nup
innotuit; qd ad uos e
rat lator pſentiū triſti
tur. Gautus̄ g diuini

ſolatiū qd in tutis aurib; liceat an
gtiarī cumulū deplorare S; unde
ſumeḡ exordiū· Ha dicendi partū
inopiā· matia copioſa & exubant.
& q̄ viſi tēpe r̄o malitia extreuiſ
ſet ad ſūmū· fidē excedit· Publica

asserting his overlordship of Brittany. Then in 1159 he launched a major campaign against Toulouse, a county he claimed was rightfully part of his wife's inheritance. But outside the walls of Toulouse Henry suffered his first real setback. King Louis hurried to support his brother-in-law the Count of Toulouse, and, rather than attack his overlord Henry, decided to withdraw. It did not take him long to get his own back. In 1158 he had betrothed his eldest surviving son Henry to Margaret, Louis VII's daughter by his second wife. Her dowry was to be the Vexin castles so long disputed between France and Normandy but as she was only six months old at the time of the betrothal Louis naturally did not expect to see the Vexin in Henry's hands for many years to come. In 1159, however, there was a disputed election to the papacy and as the price for agreeing to accept Alexander III as the rightful Pope, Henry persuaded Alexander's legates to marry the two children in November 1160. Louis VII was furious but there was nothing he could do about it.

A few months later Archbishop Theobald of Canterbury died. The see was kept vacant for more than a year and then, in June 1162, Thomas Becket was consecrated as his successor. In the eyes of respectable churchmen Becket, who had been Chancellor since 1155, did not deserve to be Archbishop. He was too worldly and too much the King's friend. Wounded in his self-esteem Becket set out to prove, to an astonished world, that he was the best of all possible archbishops. Right from the start he went out of his way to oppose the King who, chiefly out of friendship, had made him an archbishop. Inevitably it was not long before Henry began to react like a man betrayed. In the mid-twelfth century Church–state relations bristled with problems which could be, and normally were, shelved by men of goodwill but which could provide a field-day for men who were determined to quarrel. Henry chose the question of criminous clerks as the issue on which to settle accounts with his Archbishop. Like many laymen Henry resented the way in which clerks who committed felonies could escape capital punishment by claiming trial in an ecclesiastical court. At a council held at Westminster in October 1163 Henry demanded that criminous clerks should be unfrocked by the Church and handed over to the lay courts for punishment. In opposing this Becket carried his episcopal colleagues with him in defence of the privileges of their order, but when Pope Alexander III asked him to adopt a more conciliatory line he indicated his willingness to do so. In order to press home his advantage Henry summoned a council to Clarendon (January 1164). He presented the bishops with a clear statement of the King's customary rights over the church – the Constitutions of Clarendon – and required from them a promise to observe these customs in good faith. Taken by surprise Becket argued for two days and then gave in. But no sooner had the rest of the bishops followed his example than Becket repented of his weakness. Thoroughly exasperated, Henry now decided to break Becket. He summoned him before the royal court to answer trumped-up charges. The Archbishop was found guilty and sentenced to the forfeiture of all his estates. In a hopeless position Becket fled across the Channel and appealed to the Pope for protection. By taking a stand on principle and then wavering, Becket had reduced the English Church to confusion.

Once he had succeeded in driving Becket into exile Henry concentrated on more important matters for the next five years: Brittany was conquered and the English judicial system overhauled. Then in 1169 the question of the coronation of the heir to the throne, Prince Henry, led to the interminable negotiations between the King, the Pope and the Archbishop being treated as a matter of urgency. In 1170 Becket returned to England determined to punish those who had taken part in the Young King's coronation. His enemies lost no time in telling Henry of the Archbishop's ostentatious behaviour. 'Will no one rid me of this turbulent priest?' Henry's heated words were taken all too literally by four of his knights. Anxious to win the King's favour they rushed off to Canterbury; and there, on 29 December 1170, Becket was murdered in his own cathedral. The deed shocked Christendom and secured Becket's canonisation in record time. In popular memory the Archbishop came to symbolise resistance to the oppressive authority of the state, but in reality everyone, churchmen as well as princes, was better off with him out of the way. Once the immediate storm of protest had died down it became apparent that the King's hold on the resources of his vast empire had in no way been shaken by the Becket controversy. In the early 1170s Henry stood at the height of his power.

The real threat to Henry's position was to come from within his own family. The Angevin Empire was a family possession, not an indivisible state. Henry had no hesitation in planning to partition it among his sons. But his schemes aroused expectations which, while he retained all power in his own hands, he could not satisfy. For example, the Young King (in the whole of English history the only heir to the throne crowned during his father's lifetime) wanted something more than just a royal title. Thus from 1173 onwards Henry was plagued by rebellious

sons. Each new scheme caused new discontents since there was always at least one son who felt hard done by. The rebels, moreover, could always count on a warm welcome at the court of the King of France. After 1180 this was a serious matter for in that year the mild-mannered Louis VII was succeeded by his son Philip II, a shrewd and unscrupulous politician who was determined to destroy the Angevin Empire. The deaths of two of his sons, the Young King Henry in 1183 and Geoffrey in 1186, ought to have simplified Henry's problems, but this was offset by the old King's obvious preference for John, a preference which alarmed Richard. In the autumn of 1188 Richard and Philip came to terms. Throughout the winter the King's health deteriorated and by next summer he was in no condition to resist their invasion. On 4 July 1189 he was forced to accept a humiliating peace. When he was given a list of those who had fought against him he was shocked to find John's name on it. For John's sake he had pushed Richard to the point of rebellion and now John had silently joined the winning side. On 6 July the old King died at Chinon.

Only in the last weeks of his life had the task of ruling his immense territories been too much for Henry. A man of boundless energy, he rode ceaselessly from one corner of his empire to another. He travelled so fast that he gave the impression of being everywhere at once – an impression which helped to keep men loyal. He never seemed to be still; when he was not working, he was out hunting. He cared little for appearances; he dressed simply and enjoyed plain food. Although the central government offices, the Chancery, the Chamber and the Constabulary, travelled around with him, the sheer size of the empire inevitably stimulated the growth of localised administrations which could deal with routine matters of justice and finance in his absence. In England, where there was a strong administrative tradition going back to Anglo-Saxon days, government became increasingly complex and bureaucratic.

This development, taken together with Henry's interest in rational reform, has led to him being regarded as the founder of the English common law, and as a great and creative king. There is much to be said for this view of Henry, but in his own eyes these matters were of secondary importance – whatever their consequences in the long run may have been. To him what really mattered was family politics and he died believing that he had failed. But for over thirty years he had succeeded.

Opposite: The tomb of Henry II, built of polychrome stone, in the Abbey of Nôtre-Dame-de-Fontevraud.

RICHARD I *r.* 1189-99

RICHARD, THE SECOND SURVIVING son of Henry II and Eleanor of Aquitaine, was born on 8 September 1157. He spent most of his youth at his mother's court at Poitiers - a court famous for its troubadours and their songs of chivalry and courtly love. Here he was sufficiently well educated to be able to speak Latin and to write verse in French and Provençal. But above all he was educated in the art of war. To this end he took an active part in tournaments and knightly exercises.

In 1169 he did homage to Louis VII for Aquitaine and was betrothed to the French King's daughter, Alice. As the second son Richard was to have his mother's inheritance while the patrimony was to go to his elder brother. But Henry II was still only in his thirties and had no intention of allowing his young sons to govern for themselves. Frustrated, Henry, Richard and Geoffrey rebelled in 1173. In May 1174 Richard took command of his first serious campaign but at the age of sixteen he was still no match for his father and was soon forced to ask pardon. For the next few years Richard concentrated on bringing to heel the unruly barons of Aquitaine. The unstable political situation and numerous hilltop castles made it a hard school of warfare, but Richard came out of the course with flying colours. In 1183 the Young King died leaving Richard as heir to the throne. Henry II hoped that Richard would be willing to pass Aquitaine on to John, but Richard had spent too long subduing Aquitaine to give it up now. Whenever these tensions flared up into open hostility, Richard could count on the support of the new King of France, Philip II. In the summer of 1189 Richard and Philip battered Henry II into submission, and, in his moment of defeat, the old King died. On 3 September 1189 Richard was crowned at Westminster.

rdiam suam: t node canneū eius.
pud me oraeio deo uite mee: di
m deo suscepto meus es.

He stayed in England only long enough to make the necessary financial arrangements for his crusade. In 1187, under the impact of the news of Saladin's advance into the Holy Land, he had taken the Cross. For two years family feuds had prevented him from going on crusade and he was impatient to be off. He and Philip II agreed to travel together and to divide equally any conquests they might make. They set out in the summer of 1190 but transport difficulties led to the decision to spend the coming winter in Sicily. Not surprisingly, the new King of Sicily, Tancred, was somewhat alarmed by the prospect of having a large army encamped for months outside the walls of Messina, but since they were crusaders he could hardly deny them. He and Richard were not on the best of terms. Richard felt that Tancred had been less than just in his treatment of Richard's sister Joan, the widow of the previous King

Two knights jousting, from the Luttrell Psalter of 1340. The knight on the left bears the arms of Richard I; the shield of the knight on the right represents the infidel Saladin.

A page from a Latin
chronicle describing the
coronation of Richard I.

of Sicily. When fighting broke out between the crusaders and the people of Messina Richard stepped in and took the city by storm. He now held a counter with which to bargain with Tancred and he exacted very profitable terms from the hapless Sicilian. But during the enforced idleness of that winter Richard and Philip quarrelled. In Philip's view it was high time that Richard married his sister, Alice of France, but Richard, who may have believed that the girl had been his father's mistress, refused. His mother then arrived in Sicily with an alternative bride, Berengaria of Navarre, so in anger Philip sailed on ahead to the Holy Land.

When Richard left Sicily (April 1191) he took Berengaria and Joan with him. Unfortunately the ship carrying the two Princesses became separated from the main fleet and was nearly captured by the Greek ruler of Cyprus. Richard came up in the nick of time and then became involved in fighting which ended, less than a month later, with the whole of Cyprus in his hands. Militarily it was a brilliantly successful operation; strategically Cyprus was to be invaluable to future generations of crusaders. While at Limassol the wedding of Richard and Berengaria took place. Early in June 1191 Richard completed the short sea trip from Cyprus to Acre where a Muslim garrison had been under siege since August 1189. The army outside Acre was the only Christian force of any size in the whole of Outremer, yet it was itself hemmed in by a still larger Muslim army commanded by the great Saladin. If there was to be any hope of recovering Jerusalem it would first of all depend upon the outcome of the siege of Acre. Encouraged by Richard's arrival the besiegers pressed harder and a month later Acre fell. The moment of triumph was, however, clouded by the quarrel over the spoils which broke out between Richard and Duke Leopold of Austria. The crusaders suffered a further setback when Philip decided to return home.

Richard ordered the slaughter of prisoners taken at Acre and then led the army down the coast to Jaffa. They were harassed all the way by Saladin's troops even though Richard did manage to relieve the pressure slightly when he won a fine victory at Arsuf. From Jaffa it was possible to advance cautiously inland towards Jerusalem. But neither then in January 1192, nor later in June 1192, could the crusaders come any nearer to the Holy City than Beit Nuba, some twelve miles away. Richard's crusade ended when he and Saladin made a three years' truce in September 1192. Inasmuch as Jerusalem had not been recaptured the crusade had failed. On the other hand

Richard had probably done as much as was possible. The reconquest of the coastal strip and the settlement of the chaotic political affairs of the kingdom of Jerusalem were unquestionably very considerable military and diplomatic achievements.

Disturbing news from home had forced Richard to curtail his crusade and return as quickly as possible. But a combination of shipwreck and anxiety to be on his way ended with the King falling into the hands of Leopold of Austria in December 1192. For more than a year Richard remained in prison while kings and princes bargained for possession of his person. Eventually the Regents of England were able to free him in return for a ransom of £100,000, but not before his treacherous brother John had joined forces with King Philip. As a result some of the most important castles on the borders of Normandy and Touraine were lost. After a second brief visit to England from March to May 1194, Richard devoted the next five years to the hard grind of recovering the territory lost so rapidly while he was in prison. By 1199 this had been accomplished, and with the building of fortresses like Château Gaillard the defences of Normandy were in better shape than ever. Richard had won back the initiative against Philip when, in an obscure sideshow at the little castle of Chalus in the Limousin, he received a fatal wound. On 6 April 1199 he died.

His nearest male relative was his brother John, for his marriage to Berengaria had been unsuccessful and he had left no legitimate children. By the standards of his own day he had been an ideal king, preoccupied above all with the crusade and the defence of his ancestral lands. For this reason he spent only a few months of his reign in England. Unlike his father and younger brother he was uninterested in the judicial and financial detail of government, but on his return from Germany he found a minister of outstanding ability, Hubert Walter, Justiciar and Archbishop of Canterbury, a man who stood for harmonious co-operation between Church and state. In Hubert Walter's hands the domestic business of the empire was efficiently and profitably administered. It was he who raised the money to pay for Richard's ransom and Richard's wars – and vast sums were needed. A generous lord and a shrewd politician Richard was, above all else, a great soldier. His own individual prowess on the battlefield was an inspiration to his men. In the end his indifference to his own safety cost him his life, yet it was precisely this reckless quality which added the attributes of legendary heroism to a man who was also a competent king and a prudent general.

Opposite: The grave of Richard I in the Abbey of Nôtre-Dame-de-Fontevraud. The great castles that the king built stand with this effigy as his memorials.

JOHN *r.* 1199–1216

OHN WAS BORN ON CHRISTMAS EVE 1167, the last of the children born to Henry II and Eleanor of Aquitaine. After his birth his parents drifted apart. He was brought up partly in the household of his eldest brother, so that he could learn to be a knight, and partly in the household of his father's Justiciar, Ranulf Glanvil, presumably in order to learn something of the business of government. As the fourth son it was not easy to provide for him, thus the nickname 'Lackland'. Henry II's attempts to remedy this situation usually drove one or more of his other sons into rebellion. Richard's refusal to hand over Aquitaine in 1184 led to the first armed clash between John and his elder brother. Not surprisingly John came off much the worse. Then the old King devised a more promising scheme. In 1185 he sent John to rule Ireland, but although none of John's brothers had any prior rights to Ireland, the expedition ended in fiasco within six months. John and the other, equally frivolous, young men in his train were out of their depth. They rapidly alienated both the native Irish and those Anglo-Norman conquistadors who were in the process of carving out new lordships for themselves. In September 1185 John crawled back home, blaming others for his failure.

Despite everything which his affectionate father had done for him, John seems to have been in no way grateful. When, in 1189, it at last became clear that the old King was a beaten man, John secretly and cynically betrayed him, bringing despair as well as defeat to his father's last days. Then, in the hope of keeping him quiet while he was away on crusade, Richard gave him vast estates: the Norman county of Mortain, the honour of Lancaster, the revenues of six English counties, and the heiress to the earldom of Gloucester. The bribe did not work. As soon

Opposite: A fourteenth-century illuminated manuscript of King John at a stag hunt. In youth John had a reputation for frivolity and he was treacherous to his father. However, he was preoccupied with detail a nd he paid close attention to administration and the activities of the law courts in his kingdom.

Neustria Iohis fuit inde fensa sub annis
Qum pdeliquit · gallis possessa reliquit

Iohannes rex genuit videlicet

Pope Innocent III, who in 1208 suspended all church services in England and Wales for six years, following a disputed election to the see of Canterbury.

as Richard was at a safe distance John began scheming to overthrow William Longchamp, the man whom Richard had placed in charge of the administration. But news of these intrigues reached Richard while he was in Sicily and he sent back Walter of Coutances, Archbishop of Rouen, to investigate and if necessary to take over. To John's dismay this is precisely what Walter of Coutances did and by October 1191 John, who had enjoyed himself as leader of the opposition to an unpopular minister, found himself left out in the cold.

He began to conspire with King Philip of France. Their discussions began to have a real point when they heard that Richard was a prisoner in Germany. John went to Paris to do homage to Philip and then returned to stir up rebellion in England, while Philip launched his armies against Normandy. John's revolt went badly yet he still hoped for success, indeed he and Philip nearly persuaded the German Emperor to sell them Richard for £100,000.

But in February 1194 Richard was released and John was forced to sue for pardon. It was granted at once, casually and contemptuously. 'Don't be afraid, John. You are a child. You have got into bad company and it is those who have led you astray who will be punished.' (The 'child' was now twenty-seven years old.) For the next five years John remained very much in his brother's shadow, but he conducted himself well enough for the dying King to nominate him as his heir in April 1199.

Richard's wishes were respected in England and Normandy, but not in Anjou, Maine and Touraine. There the local barons chose John's twelve-year-old nephew, Arthur of Brittany, as their lord. John had to pay a high price in order to persuade King Philip to abandon the young Prince but by May 1200 he had ousted Arthur and was lord of all the Angevin dominions. Later that year he had his marriage to Isabella of Gloucester annulled and married instead Isabella of Angoulême, an heiress whose estates would help to knit together the northern and southern parts of his empire. Yet this apparently sensible marriage set in train the events which were to lead to the loss of Normandy. Isabella had been betrothed to Hugh of Lusignan; he protested against the sudden loss of his fiancée and when he got no justice from John he appealed to the court of King Philip. When John refused to answer Philip's summons, the French King declared all of his continental fiefs forfeit in April 1202.

It now remained to carry out the sentence, but at first John put up a stiffer resistance than had been expected. Indeed, by displaying an astonishing turn of speed he was able to capture Arthur of Brittany and several of the leading rebels, including the Lusignans. Arthur vanished into one of John's prisons, never to emerge again. Men had already learned to distrust John and as rumours of Arthur's fate began to percolate through Normandy and Anjou, the suspicion and the fear mounted. In this atmosphere no effective defence was possible. In December 1203 John abandoned the attempt and crossed over to England, leaving his castellans to make the best terms they could. By spring 1205 the last of his strongholds in Normandy and Anjou had fallen; Poitou also stood on the verge of surrender. These humiliating military reverses earned for John a new nickname; he became 'Soft-sword'.

From now on John's one overriding aim was to recover the lost territories. An expedition to Poitou in 1206 proved sufficient to stop the slide, but also showed John that it would require careful preparation and an immense concentration of resources before he could tackle the French King directly. For the next eight years he made his preparations, and force of circumstances meant that most of the work was carried out in England. Not since 1066 had a king of England spent so long in the country. The weight of John's presence was even felt in the north where men were not accustomed to seeing English kings. The extent of their resentment can be measured by the number of northerners who opposed John in 1215–16. But it was not just in the north that John's rule seemed to be oppressive. Scutage, which had been levied eleven times in the forty-five years between 1154 and 1199, was imposed eleven times in the sixteen years up to 1215. A recently devised tax on rents and

The head of the effigy of King John on his tomb in Worcester Cathedral.

chattels brought in huge sums. Levied at the rate of one thirteenth it yielded £60,000 in 1207 – perhaps twice the total annual revenue of the Crown in the twelfth century. The forest laws were tightened up, and also proved very profitable. The King was exerting more pressure than ever before – and all this at a time of economic and social uncertainty when prices were rising at a rate never before experienced. Many families and religious houses were in deep financial trouble and they found it easier to blame the King than to understand the underlying economic forces.

The tension spilled over into the sphere of Church–state relationships. A disputed election to the see of Canterbury in 1205 led to a clash between John and the most masterful of popes, Innocent III. In 1208 Innocent laid an interdict on England and Wales; all church services were suspended and remained so for six years. In 1209 John himself was excommunicated. Neither John nor lay society in general seems to have been very worried by this state of affairs; indeed since John's response to the interdict was to confiscate the estates of the Church it even helped to ease his financial problem. But in 1212 a baronial plot and Philip's plans to cross the Channel served to remind John that an excommunicated king was particularly vulnerable to rebellion and invasion. So he decided to make peace with the Church in order to have a free hand to deal with his more dangerous enemies. By agreeing to hold England as fief of the papacy in May 1213 he completely won over Innocent and assured himself of the Pope's support in the coming struggles.

All now turned on the result of the two-pronged attack on Philip launched by John and his heavily subsidised allies in 1214. At first all went according to plan but then, in July 1214, Philip won the vital battle of Bouvines. When news of this defeat reached England discontent turned to rebellion. Only success in war could have justified the measures which John had taken in the last eight years, and that success was still denied him. In May 1215 the rebels captured London, forcing John to make peace. In June, at a meeting with the rebel lords at Runnymede, he agreed to the terms laid out in a document later to be known as Magna Carta. In essence it was a hostile commentary on some of the more objectionable features of the last sixty years of Angevin rule – and as such clearly unacceptable to John who regarded it merely as a way of buying time. The attempts to implement the terms of this peace treaty only led, in fact, to further quarrels and the renewal of war. Seeing that they could get no more from John the rebels elected Louis of France, King Philip's son, as an anti-king of their own. In May 1216 Louis invaded and made an unopposed entry into London. When John died in October, the country was torn in two by a civil war which was going badly for the Angevins.

John possessed some good qualities. Few kings took such a close interest in the details of administration and the daily business of the law courts, but in his own day this counted for very little. John was suspicious of other men and they of him. He inspired neither affection nor loyalty and once he had shown that, no matter how hard he tried, he lacked Richard's ability to command victory in war, then he was lost. 'No man may ever trust him', wrote the troubadour Bertrand de Born, 'for his heart is soft and cowardly.' Not even the Angevin governmental machine could sustain him against that damning verdict.

THE PLANTAGENETS

1216-1399

HENRY III 1216-72

EDWARD I 1272-1307

EDWARD II 1307-27

EDWARD III 1327-77

RICHARD II 1377-99

Opposite: Edward III, depicted here receiving a sword from
St George, carefully cultivated the knightly image enshrined in
the cult of St George and King Arthur.

THE PLANTAGENETS

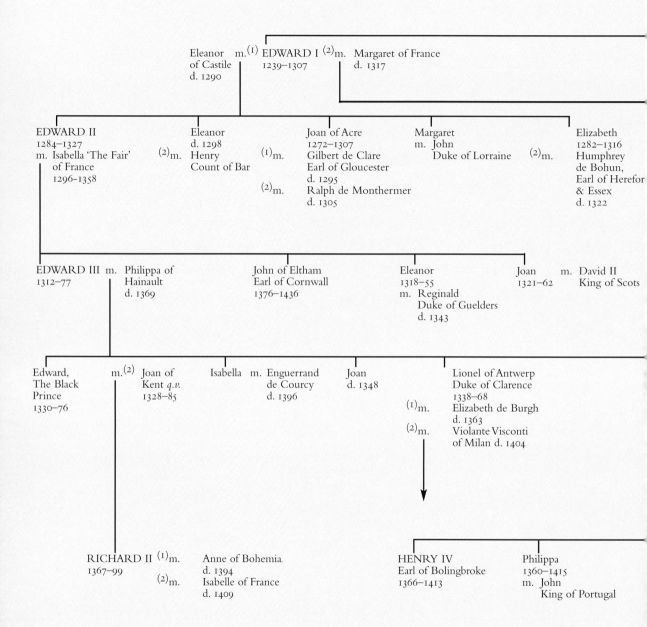

Eleanor m. (1) EDWARD I (2) m. Margaret of France
of Castile   1239–1307   d. 1317
d. 1290

EDWARD II   Eleanor   Joan of Acre   Margaret   Elizabeth
1284–1327   d. 1298   1272–1307   m. John   1282–1316
m. Isabella 'The Fair'   (2) m. Henry   (1) m. Gilbert de Clare   Duke of Lorraine   (2) m. Humphrey
   of France   Count of Bar   Earl of Gloucester   de Bohun,
   1296–1358   d. 1295   Earl of Herefor
                    (2) m. Ralph de Monthermer   & Essex
                    d. 1305   d. 1322

EDWARD III m. Philippa of   John of Eltham   Eleanor   Joan   m. David II
1312–77   Hainault   Earl of Cornwall   1318–55   1321–62   King of Scots
         d. 1369   1376–1436   m. Reginald
                              Duke of Guelders
                              d. 1343

Edward,   m. (2) Joan of   Isabella m. Enguerrand   Joan   Lionel of Antwerp
The Black   Kent q.v.   de Courcy   d. 1348   Duke of Clarence
Prince   1328–85   d. 1396   1338–68
1330–76   (1) m. Elizabeth de Burgh
                                       d. 1363
                                       (2) m. Violante Visconti
                                         of Milan d. 1404

RICHARD II (1) m. Anne of Bohemia.   HENRY IV   Philippa
1367–99   d. 1394   Earl of Bolingbroke   1360–1415
       (2) m. Isabelle of France   1366–1413   m. John
            d. 1409   King of Portugal

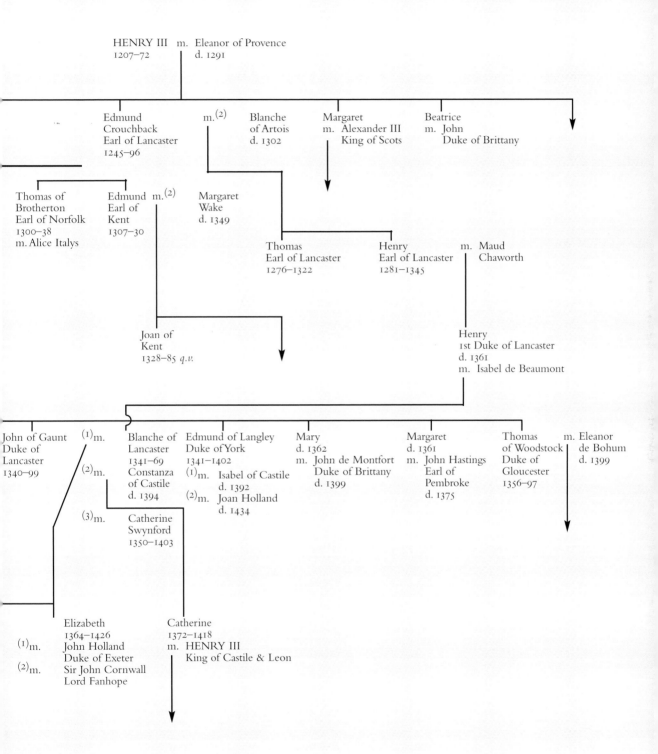

HENRY III m. Eleanor of Provence
1207–72 d. 1291

m.(2)

Edmund
Crouchback
Earl of Lancaster
1245–96

Blanche
of Artois
d. 1302

Margaret
m. Alexander III
King of Scots

Beatrice
m. John
Duke of Brittany

Thomas of
Brotherton
Earl of Norfolk
1300–38
m. Alice Italys

Edmund m.(2)
Earl of
Kent
1307–30

Margaret
Wake
d. 1349

Thomas
Earl of Lancaster
1276–1322

Henry
Earl of Lancaster
1281–1345

m. Maud
Chaworth

Joan of
Kent
1328–85 q.v.

Henry
1st Duke of Lancaster
d. 1361
m. Isabel de Beaumont

John of Gaunt
Duke of
Lancaster
1340–99

(1)m.

(2)m.

(3)m.

Blanche of
Lancaster
1341–69

Constanza
of Castile
d. 1394

Catherine
Swynford
1350–1403

Edmund of Langley
Duke of York
1341–1402
(1)m. Isabel of Castile
d. 1392
(2)m. Joan Holland
d. 1434

Mary
d. 1362
m. John de Montfort
Duke of Brittany
d. 1399

Margaret
d. 1361
m. John Hastings
Earl of
Pembroke
d. 1375

Thomas m. Eleanor
of Woodstock de Bohum
Duke of d. 1399
Gloucester
1356–97

Elizabeth
1364–1426
(1)m. John Holland
Duke of Exeter
(2)m. Sir John Cornwall
Lord Fanhope

Catherine
1372–1418
m. HENRY III
King of Castile & Leon

THE ARMS OF EDWARD III
AND RICHARD II

Opposite are illustrated the arms of Edward III (top) and Richard II. It will at once be apparent that a new element has been introduced into the simple heraldry of their predecessors. This is the crest.

At the beginning of the fourteenth century it became fashionable to have a modelled device affixed to the top of the helm. This was called the crest. It was not long before this, like the arms, came to be regarded as a hereditary symbol. When a man's full armorial bearings were displayed, as in a picture or on a seal, it became customary to show the arms on the shield surmounted by the crest on the helm. As the helm had a short cloak or mantle attached to it, possibly to deaden the effect of sword blows on the neck, this too was depicted. It is referred to as the 'mantling'.

The third seal of Edward III shows an equestrian figure with a crested helm. The crest is a golden lion *statant* (standing, as opposed to walking) *guardant*, crowned with an open crown and standing within a chapeau. The chapeau is an ancient cap of dignity, the royal chapeau being of crimson velvet lined with ermine. The royal mantling was also red and ermine.

It may seem curious that the lion in the crest is *guardant*, whereas if modelled in the round it would naturally look forward over the front of the helm. This must be regarded as early artistic licence. The seal engraver must have wanted the lion to look as it did in the arms and so committed a solecism which has continued down the centuries. In fact, as the helm of Edward, Prince of Wales, the eldest son of Edward III, has been preserved at Canterbury Cathedral, we know that in reality the lion looked forward and not over his shoulder as he does symbolically in heraldry.

In 1337 Edward laid claim to the throne of France. He symbolised this claim in his royal style, *Rex Angliae et Franciae*, and by assuming the blue field powdered with gold fleurs-de-lys, which was the arms of France. He quartered his shield and placed the French arms in the first and last (France was the senior kingdom in the medieval hierarchy) and the English in the second and third quarters.

I have mentioned that Richard II used the attributed arms of St Edward. This he did in personal rather than formal representations and in the manner illustrated.

HENRY III *r. 1216-72*

ENRY III, WHO SUCCEEDED HIS father John as King of England in 1216, inherited, apart from a passion for lampreys and a perhaps connected tendency to plumpness, a very disorganised kingdom. Much of the magnificent Angevin Empire of his grandfather Henry II had disappeared in the reign of his father, and in England itself the nine-year-old boy could claim little as his own. London and most of the south-east was in the hands of the French Dauphin Louis, while much of the north of the country was occupied by rebellious barons. Only in the south-west and a broad belt of the Midlands were there supporters prepared to recognise the child as King. Yet within a year he was undisputed King of England and at his death fifty-six years later he was to leave to his son a kingdom more united, more prosperous and more prepared to accept the rule of an autocratic king than anyone in 1216 could have imagined possible. And this in spite of the fact that he has been almost universally castigated by historians as fickle, cowardly, incompetent and totally lacking in wise judgement. Indeed most writers are happy to describe Henry in Dante's words as 'the simple king who sat apart' and then to hurry on to his more glorious son, Edward I.

Henry's ultimate success owes little to his own character. He maintained his kingdom as a boy because he had good men to help him and he handed over a strong kingdom to his son because, in the long run, most people preferred a legitimate king to anarchy or usurpation, and because virtually every institution and everybody with any real power in thirteenth-century Europe was behind him. The English had not yet acquired that remarkable habit of killing their kings in the name of progress and good government which was to make them so notorious

Opposite: Illuminated manuscript of the crowned Henry III. Henry was a cultivated mornarch who commissioned the creation of a significant number of ecclesiastical buildings, most notably Westminster Abbey. He is shown holding one of his churches.

Apres son regna henry le terz sun fiz. lvi. aunz. il
fuit de .ix. aunz de age quant fuit corone. E en son
tens fuit la bataylle de Euesham. ou fuit occys syr
Symund de munfort. e sun fiz henry. e syre hugh le de
penser e muz des barons e des cheualers de Engle
tere. puis mourst cyl henry le roy. e gist a Westmuster.

to later generations of Europeans, and although it is with Charles I that it is easiest to compare Henry III, he was never in any danger of suffering his descendant's fate.

Even in 1216 when the boy was crowned at Gloucester with his mother's chaplet, things were not as bad as they seemed. The death of King John had taken much of the point out of the baronial revolt and had made the Dauphin's presence in the country take on the appearance of a usurpation. The Pope and the Church were on the young King's side and crusading vows could be commuted to fighting to restore his inheritance. And the boy King had good men to fight for him. Foremost amongst these was the aged and loyal William the Marshal, now in his seventies, who swore when he agreed to take on the office of Rector of the kingdom that 'if need be, he would carry the King on his shoulders from land to land, rather than give in'. But this was not to be necessary. In two battles, one at Lincoln and the other at sea off Sandwich, William and the Justiciar, Hubert de Burgh, were able to destroy the opposition. The subsequent Treaty of Kingston provided for a general amnesty, very liberal terms for the former rebels and a handsome bribe to the Dauphin to leave the country.

The old Marshal died in 1219 and the government of the country largely devolved on Hubert de Burgh. A few years more were necessary to bring the country back to complete normality, but by 1227 when King Henry, now nineteen, declared his majority, something like a consensus had been reached by King and barons on the basis of Henry's acceptance of his father's Magna Carta.

Such agreement was not to last long. After ten years of tutelage the young King was eager to enjoy the realities of power. An opportunity came after the disgrace of Hubert de Burgh in 1232 on patently trumped-up charges. His successor was the very experienced and competent Peter des Roches, the Poitevin Bishop of Winchester, who actively encouraged the King to rule without the aid of his magnates. Very soon the great men of England had cause for alarm. No longer were they allowed access to the King; no longer was their advice sought. To make matters worse a stream of the Bishop's fellow-countrymen made their way to England to take advantage of his elevation to power. Jobs and privileges which had previously been the perquisites of Englishmen were now eagerly seized by the grasping foreigners.

Not for the last time in his reign King Henry was to discover the limits of his magnates' patience. In 1234 a united opposition and the threat of civil war led to the dismissal of Peter des Roches and the repatriation of the Poitevins. From this time on it was clear to Henry that there were limits to the exercise of autocratic rule. He might think, like most kings, that the magnates were his subjects as much as anyone else and should no more restrict his prerogative or criticise him than their own servants would them. But in fact such a view was incompatible with the decentralised nature of feudal society. No king had sufficient cash or military power under his immediate control to defy completely the desires of his greater subjects. To rule effectively a king had to lead his magnates and persuade the great council, or Parliament as it was increasingly called, that his way was the right way. A king who managed to do this had to be hard-working, strong-willed, consistent and admired.

Henry had none of these qualities. He was unmartial, untrustworthy and inconsistent, and as a result, although he kept out of serious trouble with his barons for the next quarter of a century, his rule was weak and came in for almost continuous criticism. The adjective most used by contemporaries to describe him was 'simple' and a good example of what was meant by this is the story told by an Italian Franciscan of the jester who compared Henry to Christ. The King, a very pious man, was flattered and asked the jester to explain the comparison. 'Because Our Lord was as wise at the moment of His conception as when He was thirty years old; so likewise our King is as wise now as when he was a little child' was the devastating reply.

Henry's desire to be his own master, coupled with his political weakness, led to constant squabbles with the barons, if not yet to more serious opposition. These squabbles brought out another characteristic of the King, the famous Plantagenet temper. But Henry was essentially a mild man and such outbursts were as often as not followed by equally rapid reconciliation. None the less nobody quite knew where they were and the King gave his barons ample opportunity to indulge in their natural suspicion and jealousy. At home the King's main policy, if indeed he had one, was to try to expand and make more efficient the system of administration within the royal household. In this he had some success but such activity was sure to make the barons suspicious. They disliked the secretive and inquisitive practices of the King's personal council. They also disliked its personnel, subordinate and insignificant persons rather than the King's natural-born counsellors – themselves. They hated even more the enormous number of foreigners who surrounded the King and seemed to monopolise all the favours being distributed, while remaining apparently immune from the law of the land.

Many of these foreigners were the kinsfolk of the Queen. Henry married Eleanor of Provence, the younger sister of the Queen of France, in 1236. Their family life seems to have been a very happy one, but the union brought problems for the English baronage. For the Queen's relatives, finding no joy at the court of the prudent Queen Blanche of France, swarmed over to England to make their fortunes. They were joined by the King's half-brothers, the children of his mother's second marriage to a Frenchman. Indeed, mid-thirteenth-century England appears to have been almost proverbial as the place to make one's fortune, replacing that former sanctuary for younger sons, the Holy Land, now reconquered by the Muslims. In such circumstances the hospitable and cosmopolitan King Henry who was so fond of his kins-folk must have seemed a godsend.

The English baronage resented competing with high-born foreign-ers and low-born bureaucrats, and grumbled accordingly. The standard way of avoiding trouble from discontented barons was to lead them to war, but Henry was a poor soldier and his tendency to lose battles did little to attract the fighting men of England to his standard. He did make somewhat desultory attempts to recover what his father had lost of the great Angevin Empire, but the complex series of truces, alliances with ambitious nobles in western and southern France, and occasional expe-ditionary forces were of no avail against the expansionist policies of the French monarchy. Finally, in 1259, Henry ratified the Treaty of Paris by which he renounced all his rights in Normandy, Maine and Anjou. He retained Gascony but only as a fief held from the King of France to whom he was bound to do homage. Further afield Henry was no more successful. He took the Cross in 1250 but was not destined to emulate the feats of his uncle, Richard Coeur-de-Lion, nor indeed of his sainted contemporary Louis IX of France, in that year a prisoner of the Saracens in Egypt. The money raised for Henry's crusade was diverted to an unrealistic and ultimately unsuccessful attempt to acquire the kingdom of Sicily for his second son, Edmund. Sicily finally went to one of the greatest adventurers of the age, Charles of Anjou, younger brother of St Louis, who built up an impressive if short-lived empire in the central Mediterranean. Henry was left with an enormous debt to the Pope, who had been the instigator of the Sicilian campaign, and mounting discontent among those whom the King expected to pay for his dreams.

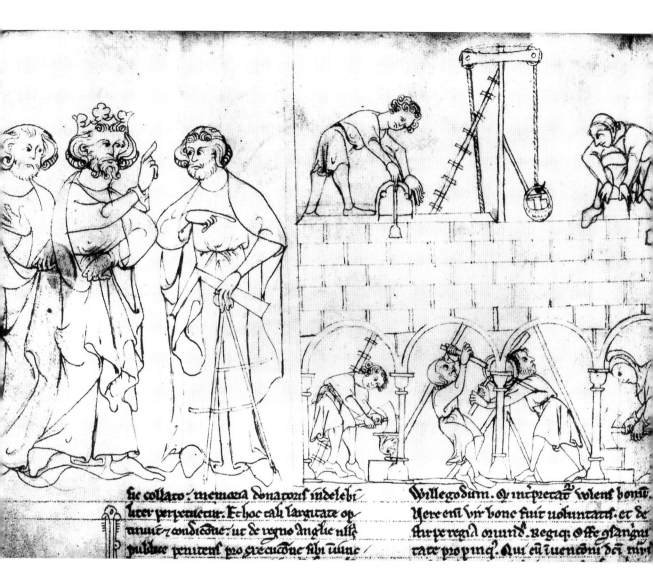

sic collato; memoria donatoris indelebi
liter perpetuetur. Et hoc tali largitate op
tinuit; conditione; ut de regno Anglie nisi
pulchre penitens pro executione sibi iuine

Willegodum. Qi interpretatur volens bonu.
Here eni vir bone fuit uoluntatis. et de
stirpe regia oriund. Regiq; Offe gsangui
tate propinq. Qui eu iuencioni dei mini

If Henry's foreign adventures cost money and gained nothing, there was one field in which he did good service both to himself and to England. Henry III was the great champion of Gothic art in England, and one of the greatest of our royal connoisseurs. His most outstanding achievements are seen in the detailed instructions and records of payment to his craftsmen. Perhaps his greatest memorial was the new Westminster Abbey, built to house the shrine of his favourite saint, Edward the Confessor. A royal saint is a good advertisement for monarchy and Henry III, like Charles I, was clearly aware of the value of art

Henry III directing the construction of Westminster Abbey, his greatest memorial, built for the shrine of Edward the Confessor.

73

as propaganda. All over the country the King's builders were at work and the great majority of the royal castles underwent structural alterations during his reign. Wherever the King went his observant eye would pick out what needed to be done to improve or beautify his buildings and detailed orders would go out for the work to be put in progress. Inside, his halls and castles were becoming increasingly decorated. A common theme was the Wheel of Fortune, beloved of the thirteenth century, which was painted above the King's chair in at least two of his castles. But a study of the images which appear on tiles, stained glass, walls and furniture in King Henry's buildings shows that the King's tastes were extremely wide-ranging. Maps of the world, cities, seasons, saints, crusaders and kings, stories from the Bible and the romances of chivalry kept an army of skilled craftsmen busy for most of the reign. An order has survived from 1256 giving instructions to pay a craftsman for painting a picture of the King rescued from his rebellious subjects by his dogs; this has a certain irony in view of what the future held, and the painting itself may have given Henry a wry confidence in the early 1260s.

For by the late 1250s the fairly friendly relationship between the King and his great council was becoming increasingly strained. The main issue was the same as it had been for the last quarter of a century, the freedom of the King to choose his own councillors and be master in his own household. But now it was given a new urgency by what seemed to the barons the enormous waste and folly of the King's Sicilian adventure. In 1258 the King was compelled by the threat of force and his lack of cash to yield to the barons and he swore to submit to their advice. It was agreed that a new council, half chosen by the King and half by the magnates, should be set up to reform the state of the realm, and that Parliament should meet three times a year. The term parliament was used at this time to describe irregular gatherings of the lay and ecclesiastical lords and the King's legal advisers.

At first it looked as though the King was sincere in his submission to the barons. But in fact it seems clear that he never intended to abide by his oath and hoped that by dividing the opposition he could maintain the royal supremacy. The period between 1258 and 1265 was a see-saw as first the magnates, then the King, rose to the top in the game of power. But in the long run the King had everything on his side. The most respected ruler of his time, St Louis of France, though a genuine peacemaker keen to resolve the differences between his brother-in-law and his vassals, was too much of a king to deny royal rights. The popes, not yet the tool of party and nation that they were to be in the next century, were also clearly behind Henry. The weapons of dispensation and excommunication were powerful ones which would be used for the King and not against him. Most serious of all, the barons' cause was doomed by the inconstancy of its own members. The King needed to make little effort to divide the opposition who, with an eye to the main chance or in a genuine belief that they had gone too far, were constantly changing sides.

Much of the drama of the contest comes from the character of Simon de Montfort, who emerged as the leader of the magnates. A younger son with comparatively poor prospects, he came from France to England in his early twenties to try to make good a somewhat tenuous claim to the earldom of Leicester. Fortune smiled on Simon as on so many Frenchmen at the English court. Not only did he obtain his earldom but in 1238 was secretly married to King Henry's widowed sister. From then onwards his close relationship and his obvious abilities brought him into constant contact with the King, a contact which developed into the love-hate relationship so typical of Henry. At one moment he would be shouting at Simon, accusing him of treachery, seduction of his sister and other terrible crimes; later he would praise him for the good work he had done in his service and shower rewards upon him. The seeds of Simon's opposition to the King clearly lie in the ambition which brought him to England in the first place, but there is little doubt that he genuinely believed in the need to curb royal pretensions to absolute power and provide for a more effective process of consultation with the great of the land. The degree of popular support for Simon's cause gives some indication of the truth of the baronial claims of royal misrule and lawlessness. This was not just another sordid baronial revolt and it is an indication of both his personality and his cause that his name is remembered today by many who would be completely unable to identify the King he opposed.

The political struggle broke out into open war early in 1264 when the barons refused to accept the French King's arbitration in favour of King Henry. After early successes for the royalists, Simon rose to the peak of his power with the complete defeat and capture of the King at the battle of Lewes in June. In his year of triumph Simon held a conference of leading supporters and summoned two burgesses and two knights from a number of boroughs and shires to attend it. But success

brought on Simon much of the opprobrium formerly reserved for the King. Now it was the royalists who were able to attract support by attacking the evil customs of the government and by demonstrating the irony of a movement, one of whose main features had been an attack on aliens in high places, being led by an alien in the person of Simon de Montfort. The dramatic escape from custody of King Henry's eldest son, the Lord Edward, provided a new leader who swore in his turn to reform the realm. Desertions from Simon's cause soon followed and on 4 August 1265 came the end of the great movement. Surrounded near Evesham by the royalist forces, Simon de Montfort and his closest supporters formed a ring around their King and prepared to fight to the death. In the midst of the battle the King formed a pitiful spectacle, in danger from friend and foe alike, as Simon's men

were hacked to death and that great fighter, Simon himself, was at last brought down and decapitated.

The last years of King Henry's reign belong more to the story of his son, who after his success at Evesham took over much of the rule of the kingdom before his departure on crusade in 1270. Henry, secure now from baronial opposition, carried on with his patronage of art and his building programme and lived to see the relics of his favourite saint, Edward the Confessor, carried to their new shrine behind the altar in Westminster Abbey in October 1269. Three years later, after one of the longest reigns in English history, the old King went to join them. A rather shadowy figure as a politician, who gained no glory in war, his chief merit was to open England up to the cosmopolitan influences emanating from the continent. King Henry gloried to emulate in England the greatest of French art and architecture, and he was a great admirer of international institutions such as the papacy and the friars, who first came to England in his reign. After his death England began to be more insular, turning its back on the continent, only to return again some seventy years later as a terrifying aggressor. Perhaps we give too much glory to our martial kings and too little to those, like Henry III, who have made England a more civilised country.

A corbel head carved in stone on the outside of Westminster Abbey, which may be a portrait of Prince Edward made when the Abbey was being built.

Opposite: Henry III's effigy, in the Chapel of Edward the Confessor in Westminster Abbey, a fitting place for the Abbey's energetic patron. The king had a great interest in decoration and was a vigorous patron of the Gothic style.

EDWARD I *r. 1272–1307*

ENGLISH NATIONALIST HISTORIANS turn with relief to Edward I after discussing the reigns of Henry III and John. Here at last is a man who has the personality to prevent the thirteenth century passing away with no English glory at all. Edward was a magnificent creature, standing head and shoulders above the ordinary man of his time, healthy, athletic, with a fine head of hair and a handsome face marred only by a drooping eyelid inherited from his father. He seemed to embody all the traditional qualities of a great medieval king. If his chief delight was in war and tournaments, he was also notable as an imaginative law-maker and a just law-enforcer, as an administrator whose authority was able to make real many of his father's attempts to strengthen and improve the royal household, and as one of those kings who have pushed forward that institution so beloved of historians, the British Constitution. No wonder that he is often claimed as the greatest of the Plantagenets.

Such reputations are bound to be vulnerable to modern criticism and Edward I, like other great men, has been demoted in recent years. Much has been made of a quotation from the Song of Lewes, written during the Barons' war of his father's reign, which described him as inconstant and treacherous. 'When he is cornered', the author wrote, 'he promises anything you like, but once he has escaped he goes back on his word. The lying by which he gains his end he calls prudence; whatever he wants he holds to be lawful and thinks that there are not legal bounds to his power.' Lest this should be merely the inconstancy of youth, the rest of his career has been examined and as a result shorn of some of its nobility. Edward, 'the maker of laws and maintainer of the rights of the weak', has been indicted of manipulating the law to disinherit some of

Opposite: The funeral effigy of Eleanor of Castile in Westminster Abbey.

One of the so-called Eleanor Crosses, built in memory of his queen by the grieving Edward I at every place where her body rested on its final journey from Nottingham to Westminster.

his greatest subjects in favour of himself and his kin. Edward, the warrior, has been accused of shabby tricks in winning his battles, and Edward, the man, of lack of generosity in rewarding those most faithful to him. What seems clear from this reassessment is that Edward was not quite the god-like figure of romance, but was an extremely tough man, able to keep his contemporaries in order, and like other tough men not above a certain amount of bullying, disregard for law and desire for personal enrichment. On the other hand, he brought a period of firm and, on the whole, just government to a country which had known only too little of such things in the previous half century.

Edward was born at Westminster in 1239. All the evidence suggests that his childhood and relationship with his parents were very happy and this domestic tranquillity was repeated in his own marriage with Eleanor of Castile, which took place in 1254. Edward's court, like his father's, was orderly, with none of the grossness of some of his forebears. When Eleanor died in Nottinghamshire in 1290, Edward was to write, 'my harp is turned to mourning, in life I loved her dearly, nor can I cease to love her in death'. He vowed to raise a cross to her memory at every town where her body rested on the way to Westminster and these memorials, three of which survive, are evidence of a much tenderer side to Edward than the character normally projected by historians. The marriage was a diplomatic one to protect the southern borders of Gascony and it was in Gascony that he first took on public duties, the duchy being settled on him together with other outlying lands of the English Crown in Ireland and Wales. He showed little evidence of either military or administrative competence during this period and various stories of youthful injustice and bullying led the chronicler Matthew Paris to feel that the prospects for the future of England under his rule were gloomy. Edward did not improve his reputation during Henry III's struggle with the barons between 1258 and 1265. He changed sides twice, broke his sworn promise on more than one occasion and was at least partly responsible for the royal disaster at Lewes. Commanding the right of the royal forces he was faced by an ill-armed body of Londoners, against whom he felt he had a particular grievance, as his mother had formerly been insulted in the city. Breaking their ranks, he chased them miles up the hill outside Lewes, only to discover when he returned to the battle that the royal cause had been lost. In the following year, after escaping from the custody of the barons, he emerged as the royalist leader, and it was his quick thinking that cut off Simon de Montfort from his reinforcements and brought him to the end of his adventure in the murderous battle of Evesham. But even there the young Lord Edward sullied his honour by the unchivalrous trick of displaying as his own the banners of some baronial supporters who had recently been captured, and thus luring Simon de Montfort to his doom. After the defeat of the barons much of the work of government fell on Edward but he showed little of that leniency which had healed wounds so quickly after the defeat of the barons in Henry III's minority. Leading rebels were savagely fined, as was Edward's bête noire, the City of London, and confiscations from the de Montforts and the Earl of Derby went to build up the enormous patrimony of Edward's brother, Edmund of Lancaster.

With the kingdom secure and his ageing father safe in his royal office, Edward was free in 1270 to fulfil a long ambition and set off on crusade with the French King, St Louis. Louis himself died that same year of fever in Tunis and Edward's crusade achieved very little, but it is during his four-year absence from England that Edward's somewhat chequered youth is forgotten and he emerges with an international reputation as a great man and a fine warrior, and reputedly the 'greatest lance in the world'.

Edward received news of Henry III's death in Sicily on his way home from the Holy Land, but he made no haste to return to his inheritance, once assured of his peaceful proclamation as King. After a magnificent passage through Italy he proceeded to Paris to visit the new French King, Philip III. Here he did homage for his French lands but he phrased his submission in the vague formula 'I do you homage for all the lands which I ought to hold of you'. Twenty years of somewhat uneasy peace were to follow before a new burst of expansionist policy in France led to a fresh outbreak of warfare in Gascony. This was to cause Edward great embarrassment as it coincided with his Scottish wars. A settlement finally came after a truce in 1297 and was later confirmed by Edward's second marriage to the French King's sister, Margaret, and by the betrothal of his son, Edward of Caernarvon, to Philip's daughter, Isabella.

On 2 August 1274 Edward landed at Dover after his four years of travel and adventure. His first task was to reassert the royal authority. Commissioners were appointed to tour the whole country to obtain evidence on such matters as the abuse of the law and local power. After so many years of weak central government, they found plentiful evidence of corruption and extortion, and many royal officers, especially sheriffs, found that their careers of easy pickings had come to an end. Although Edward's inquiry was concerned with abstract justice, its main function was to determine more clearly the boundaries between royal and private power and thus to maximise both royal authority and revenue. He disliked in particular the widespread powers in private hands, with no better warrant than long custom. Edward was unable to do much about such entrenched privileges, but he was able to define the 'time immemorable', in which so many people claimed their rights had been granted, as before the accession of Richard 1. Anything granted after then needed rigid proof. All rights now had to be clearly defined and it was shown that their extension without grant was not to be tolerated. Edward followed up his investigations in the country by considerable legislative activity, mainly under the direction of his Chancellor, Robert Burnell. In doing this he was careful to carry the great council or Parliament with him and the result was a considerable extension and clarification of the law, which has earned him the somewhat inflated title of the English Justinian.

Edward's programme of reform was interrupted in 1277 by a long-standing problem of the English monarchy, trouble in Wales. Welsh independence and power depended on the control of the inaccessible area of Snowdonia and the island of Anglesey which served as a granary. From here raids could be made south and east into the more settled areas occupied by Welsh and Anglo-Norman alike. To control this potentially explosive force the King of England depended on the Marcher lords who, in their castles in South Wales and the border counties, enjoyed a state of near independence of the English Crown in return for keeping North Welsh tendencies to expansion in check. Relations between the two cultures ebbed and flowed, depending on the strength of the lords of Snowdonia, the political condition of England and the chronic state of private war existing between the Marcher lords. Edward had had a somewhat unsatisfactory apprentice-ship into the gangster politics of the region as a young man and, now that he was feeling his strength as a king, he was reluctant to allow the former state of near anarchy to continue. By the time of his accession to the throne Welsh power was in the ascendant. The Lord of Snowdonia, Llewelyn ap Gruffydd, had taken advantage of the political disturbances of the previous reign to build up a position of considerable strength and, by the Treaty of Montgomery in 1267, had been acknowl-edged as Prince of Wales and lord of nearly all the Welsh chieftains.

He now sought a greater degree of independence and refused repeatedly to do homage to Edward, on the grounds that the King had refused to hand over for justice his brother David, suspected of a plot against him. Edward, aware of the problems of Welsh campaigns, was at first reluctant to take action against this challenge to his feudal over-lordship, but in 1277 he decided to exert his authority. In a remarkably well-organised campaign he cut off the Prince from his supply base in Anglesey and forced him to surrender. The settlement was very mild. Llewelyn lost his lands outside Snowdonia and Anglesey, but retained his title as Prince of Wales.

Five years later the Welsh were up in arms again and Edward was forced to repeat his previous campaign. This time he was at first not so successful and the attempted invasion of Snowdonia from Anglesey was foiled. However, the death of Llewelyn after a skirmish led to the col-lapse of Welsh resistance and the complete conquest of North Wales. Edward took this opportunity to reorganise completely the government of this troublesome area. By the Statute of Wales of 1284, the area was transferred to the King's dominion and divided up into shires on the English pattern. Although the basis of law and custom under the new administration continued to be Welsh, those features which the English did not like were removed and in fact during the next century the whole region underwent a steady process of anglicisation. To secure his new dominion Edward ordered the building of that great ring of castles on the coast surrounding the mountains of Snowdonia that remains today as an impressive, if somewhat grim, monument to his most suc-cessful enterprise.

Edward I's successes as a general depended heavily on efficient organisation, both of supply and of recruitment. During his Welsh and Scottish wars he was able to bring into the field armies which were not to be exceeded in size in England till the Civil War of the seventeenth century. Admittedly, most of these men were infantry, poorly armed and eager to desert, but their sheer numbers were often sufficient to intimidate the enemy, and they included large numbers of Welsh archers whose skill foreshadowed the English military success of Edward III's reign. Most battles, however, were still won by cavalry, not archers. The Crown still had the right to unpaid feudal service for forty days but this was now often more of an embarrassment than an asset. Both the King and his magnates began to supplement their feudal levies with paid retainers with whom they had made contracts specifying the nature and length of service and the rate of pay that they should receive.

Edward's wars and the large armies with which he fought them put an enormous strain on the royal revenue. His reign sees a considerable expansion of taxation which resulted, as so often in the reigns of financially embarrassed kings, in a parallel expansion of the effectiveness of the Parliaments which granted the extra taxes. Regular meetings of Parliament became an established feature of British political life in Edward's reign and sometimes knights and burgesses were summoned to attend, following the precedent set by Simon de Montfort.

However, taxation was not enough for Edward's needs. The traditional source of extra revenue was to tallage the Jews but, by Edward's reign, past extortions had so impoverished them that this was hardly worth the effort. In 1290 he killed the golden goose for good, expelling the Jews from England and seizing most of their remaining assets. Their place as royal creditors was taken by Italians, papal bankers and wool exporters, who exchanged loans for trading privileges and left Edward at his death in considerable debt.

The arena in which most of this money was spent during the last decade of Edward's reign was Scotland. Relationships between England and Scotland in the thirteenth century were similar to those between England and Wales, although the Scots had a far greater degree of real independence. None the less the King of England claimed the overlordship of the northern kingdom, a claim which at times the Scots were preprared to accept. A chance for Edward to exercise this claim, and if possible to reinforce it, came in 1286 when King Alexander III of Scotland died, leaving as heir his six-year-old granddaughter, the Maid

Opposite: An lluminated manuscript depiction of Parliament, which began to meet on a more regular basis during the reign of Edward.

longtain voyage. quil fouffira de porter feulemet vng
fac de foye a vncf ymage de fainct georgie pendat a icelluy.
Auffi fe ledit colier dor auoit befoincf de reparation il pôra
eftre mis en la main de fouuuier iufques a ce quil foit
repair. Lequel colier auffi ne pourra eftre enrichy de
pierres ou daultres chofes referue fes ymage qui pourra
eftre garny au plaifir du cheualier. Et tauffi ne pourra
eftre ledit colier vendu engaige dône ne aliene pour
neceffite ou caufe quelconque que ce foit

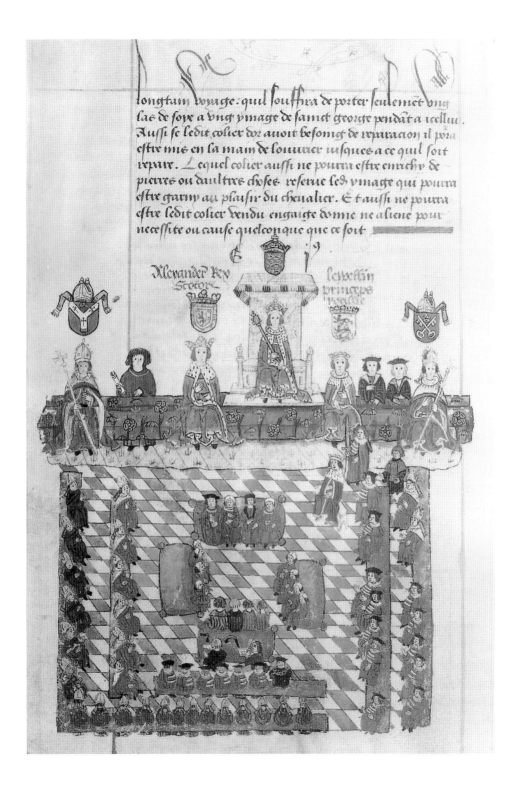

of Norway. Edward's first plan, which was accepted by the Scots and would have saved much bloodshed, was to marry the girl to his son Edward, born at Caernarvon in 1284. But sadly, in 1290, the girl died in the Orkneys on her way from Norway to Scotland, leaving the Scots with the horrors of a disputed succession. Edward, as overlord, was called in to adjudicate between the three main claimants. After careful consideration, he chose John Balliol, a decision which most historians have considered to be fair and just. What was less fair was the advantage Edward took of the needs of the Scots and the weakness of Balliol to establish his supremacy over the northern kingdom. Ultimately Edward's demands pushed the Scots into accepting in 1295 an alliance with Philip of France with whom Edward was now at war. This clever move came just a little too late. The Welsh too had tried to take advantage of Edward's troubles in France and had risen in the winter of 1295. But Edward had time to quell the Welsh rebellion and then in the spring of 1296 to strike at Scotland. Berwick was stormed and sacked by the King in March, and in late April the main Scots army was crushed by Earl Warenne of Surrey at Dunbar. Edward made a grand passage through Scotland, accepted the submission of the great men and the abdication of Balliol, seized the Stone of Destiny from Scone Abbey and was back in Berwick in August. As a contemporary put it, he 'conquered the Kingdom of Scotland and searched it through in twenty-one weeks'. He then left the country to be ruled by Earl Warenne and went home.

Edward had seriously underestimated the Scots. His contemptuous treatment of them led to bitter hatred of their English conquerors which flared up in the year after Dunbar into a war of independence which was long to outlast his reign. Such hatred was soon matched by the English who were subjected to the horrors of continuous raiding and whose instinctive dislike of their northern neighbours was fed by stories of savage atrocities.

In the face of English military superiority, much of the Scots resistance took the form of guerrilla fighting from bases in the hills and forests. The first great leader to emerge was the gigantic outlaw William Wallace, whose dramatic exploits play such a large part in Scots legend. Supported mainly by peasants and outlaws like himself, Wallace was able in 1297 to score a decisive victory over Earl Warenne at the battle of Stirling Bridge. Although Edward had his revenge in 1298, when he returned with the greatest army he had ever assembled to destroy Wallace at the battle of Falkirk, the outlaw himself was not captured till 1305 and was succeeded in the following year by a new leader who was ultimately to inflict on England the most devastating defeat in her history.

Robert Bruce was the grandson of one of the claimants to the Scots throne at the death of the Maid of Norway. Like most of the nobles he had made his peace with King Edward, but in 1306, after putting himself beyond the law by murdering a rival for the forfeit throne, he decided to make a bid for popular support and had himself crowned King of Scotland. His early career as king was a disaster and he spent most of that summer hiding in the heather from Englishman and Scot alike. But he remained alive and his threat was sufficient to force the ailing King of England to undergo one last campaign to conquer Scotland. The old King never got there. On 7 July 1307, aged sixty-eight, the 'hammer of the Scots' died at Burgh-on-Sands within sight of the Scottish border. His last command was that his son should carry his bones at the head of his armies until the last Scotsman had surrendered.

The assessment of Edward's expansionist policy depends ultimately on one's view of the benefits of the union of the whole island. Traditional English historiography, with its firm roots in the British world empire of the nineteenth century, saw such a union as part of England's manifest destiny. Today opinion is not so unanimous. Edward's legal justification for his attempt to bring both Wales and Scotland under the direct dominion of the English Crown is dubious and his failure in Scotland was to give rise to three hundred years of intermittent warfare and almost continuous border-raiding. In return for this devastation and mutual slaughter it can hardly be said that either kingdom received much benefit.

EDWARD II *r. 1307-27*

N O KING OF ENGLAND HAS HAD such a consistently bad press as Edward II. Squeezed in between his two warrior namesakes he seemed to justify contemporary suspicion that he was a changeling. Yet the outward appearance was quite clearly that of a Plantagenet. He was as tall, strong, golden-haired and good-looking as his father in his prime, but inside this magnificent shell there was no king as the fourteenth century understood that word. He made no effort to rule or impress his subjects. He cared nothing for the duties of a king. His only desire was to use the advantages of his position to enrich his friends and amuse himself. Such behaviour of course was not all that uncommon among kings, but in addition both Edward's friends and his amusements were themselves suspect. The King had no taste for jousting and the other martial pursuits of his class. Instead he preferred to test his strength in activities of a distinctly plebeian sort, such as digging or rowing, or to learn and practise the manual crafts of his subjects like thatching and farming. Today we would hardly condemn such activities with the intensity that Edward's contemporaries did, but even now they hardly fit our conception of a medieval king.

Edward compounded his faults by the low company he kept in pursuing his rural amusements. But even worse was the company he kept at court. He systematically avoided his natural counsellors, the magnates of the land, and gave his heart and all the spoils that flowed from the royal office to upstarts. Edward was a very good friend and his loyalty to his friends is one of the most attractive features of his character, but a policy of continually antagonising the magnates was certain to lead to trouble.

Opposite: Manuscript illumination of Queen Isabella in conversation with John of Hainault during her return from France to invade her husband's kingdom.

la royne dangleterre psabel
arriua en angleterre z mes
sire Jehan de haynau . xe

nsi estoit esmeu
et encouraige mo
sire Jehan de hay
nault et faisoit

Edward II holding the symbols of kingship, the orb and sceptre, and standing on a royal lion. However, he did not behave in a way thought by his contemporaries to be kingly, and he alienated many of his subjects.

The amateur psychologist which lurks within most historians has made much of Edward's upbringing to explain his unroyal behaviour, which could well have been in part the reaction of a weak son to a strong-willed and increasingly tyrannical father. If Edward I bears some responsibility for his son's character he certainly left him other problems which such a character would be unable to solve. His powerful personality had been able to subdue a serious threat to his autocracy in 1297, but there were many of the magnates who felt that the spirit of the royal concessions of the earlier thirteenth century had been forgotten and who were now only waiting for the death of the terrifying old man to impose themselves on his son. More immediate was the chaotic legacy in Scotland of a war which already looked as if it would never be won. The young King's reaction to his father's last command that he should pursue the Scottish war to the bitter end was very much in character. After a perfunctory march across the border, he gave up the north to civil war and the triumph of Robert Bruce and returned to London to enjoy himself.

Here he was joined by the best of his friends, Piers Gaveston, a handsome Gascon knight with an eye to the main chance, who had been his close companion since childhood. So extravagant were Edward's demonstrations of affection for his 'brother Perrot' that it is generally assumed that there was a homosexual relationship between the two young men. It is clear that Edward I shared these suspicions and Gaveston had twice been banished by the old King. But now there seemed nothing to stop Edward II from showing to the world how much he loved his favourite. Less than a month after Edward I's death, Gaveston was made Earl of Cornwall, a title formerly held only by

The intense personal relationship between the handsome Gascon knight Piers Gaveston and Edward II, pictured here, caused such animosity that it would lead to Gaveston's murder.

the sons of kings. Shortly afterwards he was married to the King's niece, and a further insult to the magnates came early in 1308 when the King left Gaveston as Regent when he went over to Boulogne to bring home his young bride, Isabella of France. Edward soon made it plain that the delights of marriage were not going to cool his love for Gaveston. Many of his wedding presents were given away to the favourite and at his coronation he shocked the court by demonstrating that he preferred the couch of Perrot to that of the Queen.

Gaveston did nothing to quell the hatred and jealousy that Edward's generosity aroused in the hearts of the magnates. Indeed he went out of his way to ridicule them, inventing derisive nicknames for them and, even worse, inviting them to a tournament and then demonstrating that his sword was as keen as his tongue by decisively defeating them.

Edward and Gaveston were playing a dangerous game. No king had the military resources to fly in the face of the united opposition of the earls in those days of private armies. Total unity was, of course, unlikely and the number of opponents of the King ebbed and flowed, but the King's behaviour ensured that they were usually sufficient to put very considerable pressure on him. Within a year of Edward's accession, the threat of force from a strong baronial group drove the King to agree to the exile of Gaveston. Edward made strenuous efforts to appease and divide his opponents but had to agree to a programme of reform undermining the royal prerogative before his favourite was reinstated. However, Gaveston's insufferable arrogance speedily reunited the nobility against him. A committee calling itself the Lords Ordainers enforced Edward's agreement to detailed reforms and the perpetual exile of Gaveston. But Edward had no intention of implementing anything or honouring any of his promises. All he wanted was to go on as he had before with Gaveston by his side. Within two months of his second exile the favourite appeared openly at the Christmas court at Windsor. This was too much for the earls. After a short struggle, Gaveston was captured and murdered by his enemies, despite a promise that he should be allowed to plead his case before Parliament.

In many ways the murder of Gaveston was a tactical mistake, since it removed the main focus of opposition and, by marshalling opinion against the murderers, put Edward in a stronger position than he had so far enjoyed as monarch. This royalist reaction, however, was only superficial and there still existed an opposition movement determined to reduce the King to a mere figurehead to carry out their wishes. The leader of this group and the most consistent opponent of the King was his first cousin, Thomas of Lancaster. The fortunes of his house had been built up on the confiscated estates of the de Montforts after the battle of Evesham in 1265. By 1311 Lancaster had become a classic over-mighty subject with five earldoms in his possession and an immense private army at his command. In a rather fanciful way he now saw himself as a second Simon de Montfort who would control the King in the interest of his greater subjects. There are of course parallels between the two situations but Lancaster was unfortunately no de Montfort. By all accounts he was a thoroughly nasty man, grasping and vicious, and on many occasions in his career the idealism involved in opposition to the King was tarnished by his only too obvious desire to divert the benefits that the King was giving elsewhere to himself. To make matters worse, when power did come into his hands he seemed incapable of using it, preferring to stay within his castles and leave the country in a state near to anarchy.

Lancaster's defiance of the Crown came out into the open in 1314 when he and three other earls refused to accept the King's summons to military service against Scotland, on the grounds that the expedition had not been approved by Parliament. It proved to be a wise decision. Edward had hoped to lead his disgruntled barons to a great victory and bring a little glory to his reign but his efforts brought only disaster and the triumph of the stay-at-home Lancaster. On Midsummer Day 1314, after a display of incredible incompetence by both the King and his military advisers, the English were totally defeated at the battle of Bannockburn by Robert Bruce and a Scottish army only one-third their strength. In one day Bruce had assured the independence of Scotland. Edward was to make other expeditions to Scotland but none had any real success.

The next three years must be amongst the worst in English history. After the disaster of Bannockburn, Edward II gave up even the pretence of ruling and became a mere puppet in the hands of Lancaster. But as the royal power collapsed, Lancaster did little to replace it. The Scots ravaged the north of England, levying ransoms from the towns, while private warfare broke out in many other parts of the kingdom. Providing a grim background to this situation of chaos was the worst famine in European history.

In 1318 some semblance of normality returned. A measure of reconciliation between Edward and Lancaster was engineered by the so-called middle party under the leadership of the Earl of Pembroke, the most honourable and competent of the earls. But Edward still remained a king in name only, his every act to be controlled by a standing council. None the less, by exchanging one master for many he had returned to the position of being able to play them off against each other. For, despite his weakness, Edward was still determined to reassert the royal prerogative and avenge himself on his enemies.

Any hopes that Edward had been tamed for ever were quashed by the rise of new favourites at court. The two Despensers, father and son, were Marcher lords whose greed and ambition were as great as those of Gaveston, but whose ability and sense of political responsibility were far greater. To begin with their story was a repetition of the events of the early part of the reign. Supported by the Despensers the King cast off the control of the magnates and in return for their support they were rewarded with a flow of estates and hard cash. Jealousy led to an inevitable baronial reaction, particularly from the other Marcher lords

aucecques iiii.
Comment messire huon
despensier fut Justicie.
xvie. Chapitre.

Unt la feste ru
passee les nir
huon qui vm
nestoit aime l.

who resented the expansion of the Despensers' power in South Wales. In 1321 a combination of the Marcher lords and Lancaster forced Edward to agree to the exile of the new favourites.

Here the similarity to the story of Gaveston ends. For in the following year Edward was to act with more resolution than ever before in his reign and completely break the main centres of opposition to royal power. Supported by a movement of moderate opinion in his favour, Edward was able to strike at the Marchers in Wales and force them to surrender. Then he turned his attention to Lancaster whose failure to support his allies had been the major cause of their defeat. The now isolated Lancaster ruined his chances by asking Robert Bruce to come to his aid with a Scottish army. This treachery made him a target for the hatred of the long-suffering northcountry men, who defeated what was left of Lancaster's great private army at Boroughbridge. At last Edward had the chance to revenge the murder of Gaveston ten years earlier and to pay back his cousin for the years of humiliation after Bannockburn. Lancaster's head was hacked off and the King and the returned Despensers ruled the land.

The long tale of deceit, incompetence, treachery and violence which is the story of the reign of Edward II has a fitting end. The key figure was that of the Queen, Isabella of France. We have seen how shabbily she was treated at her marriage and in the days of Gaveston, but from his death until the early 1320s there seems to have been little discord between the royal couple. They had certainly done their duty in providing for the succession. The future Edward III was born in the year of Gaveston's murder and he was followed by a second son and two daughters. The Queen herself was well looked after and her occasional interventions into politics were those of a peacemaker. But after the defeat of Lancaster in 1322 there were increasing rumours of troubles in the marriage and the Queen emerges as the focus of a new opposition movement determined to overthrow the Despensers. The Despensers returned the Queen's dislike but seem to have been too confident of their own security and power to do much to check her political ambitions. In 1325 they made a very bad mistake. Relations between England and France had once again come to a head and it was suggested that Isabella, sister of the King of France, might be the best person to re-establish peace. Edward and the Despensers unwisely agreed and the lady who became known as the 'she-wolf of France' sailed away to find her rather sordid place in the history books.

Opposite: Jean Froissart's chronicles of the exploits of the nobles of England and France include this illumination of Hugh Despenser the Younger, the Marcher lord and favourite of Edward, being brutally executed in 1326 on the orders of Queen Isabella.

Isabella's court in Paris became a centre for exiles eager to destroy the regime of the Despensers. Amongst these, one of the most powerful was Roger Mortimer, a great Marcher lord, who had been defeated by Edward II in 1322 but had later escaped from the Tower. To the horror of her brother, the King of France, Isabella openly took Mortimer as her lover and the couple prepared for the invasion of England. The Queen's position was strengthened by the arrival of her eldest son, Edward, to do homage for Aquitaine in the name of his father. Isabella now refused to allow him to return to England and openly defied Edward II and the Despensers.

In 1326 Isabella was forced to leave France as her brother was no longer prepared to put up with the scandal of her liaison with Mortimer. Undismayed, Isabella and Mortimer went to Hainault whose count was persuaded to support her cause with a body of mercenaries by the proposal that his daughter Philippa should marry the young Prince Edward. At last all preparations had been made and, on 23 September, the Queen, her son and Mortimer sailed to Suffolk to invade her husband's kingdom.

That kingdom, long tired of the rule of the King and his favourites, welcomed the Queen with open arms. There was virtually no resistance and Edward II retired with the Despensers to the main base of their strength in the west. The tragedy was slowly played out. One by one the Despensers and the other supporters of the King were captured and executed in various horrible ways.

The King himself was not so easy to deal with. After his capture on 16 November he was persuaded to hand over the great seal of England so that writs could be issued in his name for a Parliament. But Parliament without a king is no Parliament and, in order to give some semblance of legality to the deposition on which nearly everyone was set, it was necessary to persuade the King to renounce the Crown in favour of his son. Edward at this time was a well-treated prisoner of Lancaster's brother, the Earl of Leicester, at Kenilworth Castle. He put up a spirited resistance to the deputation who came to see him, but the threat that his son might be repudiated persuaded him at last to agree to the terrible demand.

The continued existence of the deposed King was an embarrassment and a threat to the Queen and Mortimer. Mortimer's solution was to have him secretly and shamefully murdered in the dungeon of Berkeley Castle. Here his gaolers, having failed to starve him to death, satisfied

their orders to leave no mark on his body by thrusting a red-hot spit into his bowels. Two months later he was buried in Gloucester Abbey in a lavish ceremony attended by both the Queen and the new King.

Edward must always arouse sympathy for the horror of his death and indeed it is easy to feel some sympathy for his whole predicament as King. He is really a standing indictment of hereditary monarchy. He clearly did not have the ability to be a king but simply because he was his father's eldest surviving son England had to endure twenty years of his reign. Since these two decades were years when the monarchy was faced with particularly difficult problems and when most of the great earldoms were filled with particularly unpleasant men, the reign of Edward II was one that most people would be glad to forget.

The tomb of Edmund Crouchback, Earl of Lancaster and the King's younger brother, who was one of the knights instrumental in the final defeat of the Scots. He went to the crusades with Edward I and his body is buried to the left of the high altar in Westminster Abbey.

EDWARD III *r.* 1327-77

ENGLAND EXPECTS HER MONARCHY to produce at least one great king each century. But even chauvinists like a surprise. Who would have thought that the pathetic Edward II, who presided over England's fortunes for two decades of military failure and baronial quarrels, could have spawned such a magnificent son? And who could have foreseen that this son, the pawn of his scandalous mother and the grasping Mortimer, would not only restore harmony to the English upper classes but would also become the greatest warrior king in Christendom who, thirty years after his accession, was to entertain two captive kings at a series of feasts which were said to be the most splendid since the days of his model, King Arthur?

Edward III was fourteen when he was crowned King of England in 1327, the first king to rule by a Parliamentary title. The child who had been born a few months after the murder of his father's favourite, Gaveston, showed no signs that he had inherited his father's low tastes. In every way he appeared to be a conventional representative of his class and there is no evidence that he had any reluctance in joining with his mother to forward his father's deposition. Later he was to make a rather half-hearted attempt to bolster up the royal dignity by building a splendid tomb over his father's grave and encouraging the cult which brought simple pilgrims to the last resting place of a king who had been brought so low, but there seems little doubt that Edward could feel little respect for the man who had brought the English monarchy to its lowest ebb.

Edward's first task was to restore once more the shattered dignity of that monarchy. At first, still a boy, he found himself under the dual control of a regency council of barons led by Henry of Lancaster and a

Opposite: Manuscript illumination of the coronation of Edward III at the age of fourteen. The son of the weak Edward II, he was destined to become the greatest warrior king in Christendom.

Dres que les pl̃z
des compaignons
de haynault se
furent partiz.

court dominated by the arrogant Mortimer, his mother's lover, who was clearly angling for the throne himself. But Edward grew up fast. By 1330 he was ready to strike. With Lancaster's connivance, the King's servants seized Mortimer at Nottingham Castle, as he lay in the Queen Mother's chamber. His supporters disappeared and he was charged before his peers in Parliament with an appalling range of crimes, of most of which he was quite clearly guilty, and executed. Isabella was forgiven and allowed to retire to live a quiet life on a reduced income at Castle Rising in Norfolk.

Following his successful coup Edward pursued a very sensible policy of toleration. There was no wholesale slaughter of Mortimer's followers and most of them were absorbed without difficulty into the life of the kingdom. Mortimer's grandson was later restored to all his grandfather's titles and was to prove a faithful supporter of the King. In this he was no exception, for everyone was a faithful supporter of Edward. It was his most remarkable achievement that he was able to turn the baronage into one great happy family with himself as their leader and their friend. It was in fact a family in more senses than one, for Edward strengthened his position by marrying many of his children to the sons and daughters of magnates, thus tying great houses such as Mortimer and Lancaster to his own dynastic ambitions.

Edward was able to keep the loyalty of his barons because for the most part his tastes were their tastes. Indeed with a diet of war, wine, women, good parties and just enough cultural activity to satisfy the more literate of his colleagues, he could hardly go wrong, especially when the wars provided victory and loot. Edward was obviously not only a great leader and a great soldier but also a superb host whose court was fully appreciated by the barons. The ethos of the court derived from the romances of chivalry and Edward took great care to promote the knightly image enshrined in the cult of St George and King Arthur. A central feature was the new-style tournament in which the formal, but still highly dangerous, single combat in the lists had replaced the mock battles of the thirteenth century. The culmination of Edward's glorification of the knight and of his promotion of baronial harmony came in 1348 with the establishment of the Knights of the Garter, whose twenty-six members were to be 'co-partners both in peace and war'.

This was no idle boast for, if Edward is remembered chiefly for his success in leading his barons to war, he was equally successful in absorbing their natural instinct for criticism of their King in the political arena.

Apart from one quickly settled constitutional crisis in 1341 when he learned the lesson that even a popular monarchy has limits, Edward achieved a remarkable record of acceptable government, combining an executive which was sufficiently independent not to make him feel unroyal, with a parliament which was consulted often enough to make its members feel that this was indeed a consultative monarchy and not a tyranny.

To be a successful knightly king it was important to succeed in war, a condition which England had not known for some time. Edward himself had been forced to sign the humiliating Treaty of Northampton in 1328, by which Robert Bruce was at last recognised to have won his long war for Scottish independence. But the great Bruce was to die the following year, leaving his son David, still a child, as King. Here was a chance to play the old game of supporting a Balliol against a Bruce. Meanwhile the standing grievance of Scots presence in the north and continued Scots raids could only be removed on the battlefield. In 1332 Edward went to York and at the end of the year lay siege to Berwick with a well-trained army. A new spirit and a new professionalism could be seen in the English and when the Scots came south to raise the siege in the following year they were convincingly defeated at the battle of Halidon Hill. Edward had avenged the military failures of his father's reign. More alarming to those who could appreciate it was the method of Edward's victory, for Halidon Hill was the first of those great victories which were to ensure English military supremacy for the next century by coupling the firepower of the archer with his longbow to the skill of the dismounted man-at-arms.

The English victory forced the Scots back into the hands of their old ally, the King of France. That pattern of encircling alliances already used so adroitly by Philip the Fair against Edward I now once again threatened English possessions both at home and abroad. Indeed there were few English possessions left abroad. Ever since Henry III had signed the Treaty of Paris in 1259 and had agreed to do homage for Gascony, the expansionist policies of the Kings of France had tended to nibble away at what remained of the great Angevin Empire. The feudal relationship implied that Gascon subjects of England had a right of appeal to the English King's overlord in Paris. If this right were accepted then the English were sure to lose in the French courts. If it were refused then such disobedience to a feudal superior could mean that Gascony itself was forfeit. By the time that Edward III came to the throne French lawyers and English weakness had reduced the English possessions in south-west France to a narrow coastal strip. Once these last lands had disappeared there was every evidence that a Franco-Scottish alliance might try to nibble away at England as well.

Dynastic accident gave Edward a chance to slip out of this feudal noose. The legal problem would at once be solved if he himself was the King of France. It so happened that the death without male heir of Charles IV in 1328 gave Edward a very respectable claim to the French throne through his mother, Charles's sister. Nothing was said at the time and Edward paid homage to Charles's cousin, Philip VI of Valois, who seized the Crown without opposition. But an English claim to the French throne was a useful background to the aggression which was being planned to recover the lost English lands in France, as well as providing a good excuse for other discontented vassals of Philip to change their allegiance. And of course the withdrawal of the English claim could be a useful bargaining counter in the future.

By 1337 Edward felt powerful enough to come out into the open. His plan was to advance into France from the north-east and defeat Philip VI in open battle. Not yet realising precisely how significant for the future his tactics at Halidon Hill were to be, Edward felt the need for an offensive alliance of princes from the east and north-east of France to support his invasion. Many of these princes were themselves the victims of French aggression and Edward's diplomacy at first appeared to have been very successful. Meanwhile a great propaganda campaign in England proclaimed that Edward had suffered unjust treatment at the hands of the French and his rightful claim to the throne of France. The support he received, both in money and men, was very encouraging and in 1338 Edward crossed over to Antwerp to round up his allies and invade France.

The results of this first stage of what was to become the Hundred Years' War were very disappointing. The only real success was a naval victory in 1340 over a combined French and Genoese fleet at Sluys. But success in the field seemed far harder to achieve. Nothing would induce Philip to come to battle. Nor would he accept Edward's chivalrous invitation to decide the issue by single combat. Meanwhile Edward's allies proved to be hideously expensive and ultimately unreliable. By 1343 it was clear that his attempt to recover his French fiefs had been a very expensive failure. The long years of disappointment ended, however, in 1345 when Henry of Derby, Edward's greatest soldier, recaptured most of Gascony in a whirlwind campaign. Much encouraged, Edward prepared a vast army to invade France.

Edward III was to encounter none of the difficulties met by his ancestors in raising armies to serve abroad. The old feudal element in the army had now been almost entirely replaced by contractual relationships made between the King and his captains. Such captains were for the most part the great of the land and they in turn had no difficulty in raising men to serve under them. The prospect of being paid to fight under so popular a king was an attractive one, soon to be made even more attractive by the realisation that English military superiority would allow them to plunder, burn and rape their way through the richest country in Europe with little danger. The reality of the *chevauchée* was a long way from the ideal of chivalry implied in the cult of King Arthur.

On 12 July 1346 Edward landed with his army of men-at-arms and bowmen on the Cotentin peninsula in Normandy. The orgy of burning and destruction which followed, as Edward moved through France's most prosperous province on his way to link up with his allies in Flanders, was too much for even Philip VI to ignore. The flower of French chivalry was summoned, the oriflamme unfurled and on 26 August Edward III, after crossing the Somme with great difficulty, was brought to bay in a defensive position at Crécy. Confident in their enormous superiority in numbers the French attacked just as the sun was beginning to set. But then 'the English archers stept forth one pace and let fly their arrows so wholly together and so thick that it seemed snow'. Attack after attack broke down under the hail of fire and the steadiness of the dismounted men-at-arms until, by midnight, there was a great wall of dead before the English lines and Philip fled from the field with the remnant of his army. It was the end of the old wars of chivalry.

After the battle Edward led his victorious army to Calais, which after a long siege surrendered in the face of starvation and thus gave the English a base for further assault much nearer to home. The final seal on English triumph came with news from the north. The Scots had taken advantage of Edward's departure to march across the border, only to be crushed by the fighting Archbishop of York, William de la Zouche, in a terrible battle in thick fog at Neville's Cross near Durham. Amongst the prisoners was King David who was taken to London as the most convincing evidence of the might of English arms.

The next three years are dominated in European history by the first onslaught of the Black Death, which is estimated by many historians to

The battle of Poitiers, from
the Froissart chronicles.
The resounding French
defeat led to the collapse of
the government and the
breakdown of law and order.

have killed one-third of the population of western Europe. The social changes brought about by such a calamity were ultimately to pose new problems for the English monarchy, but its immediate impact on the biography of Edward III was surprisingly small. Normal history did not stop in the face of such clear evidence of God's displeasure with man. The truce made after the battle of Crécy was extended till 1350, but then, with the death of Philip VI and the accession of the optimistic King John, hostilities broke out once more. The English strategy was similar to that of the Crécy campaign. Large-scale raids from both Gascony and Calais filled English pockets and at last drew the French once again to battle. This time success was to fall to the King's eldest son, Edward, the Black Prince, already at the age of twenty-six a warrior with an impressive military reputation. In 1356 he won his astonishing victory at Poitiers in which King John himself was captured and sent back to England to join King David of Scotland in captivity.

After Poitiers the government of France broke down and the country dissolved into virtual anarchy. Peace could still not be made on terms acceptable to both sides and in the winter of 1359–60 Edward III sailed to France to try to impose his will in one last terrible raid. Edward's men suffered dreadfully in what were appalling climatic conditions and the expedition was a military failure. But it was enough to force the issue. In 1360, by the Treaty of Brétigny, all Edward's original claims were satisfied. His sovereignty over Calais and the whole of Aquitaine, nearly a quarter of France, was recognised, and in return he renounced his claim to the French Crown.

This remarkable recovery of the English position in France after the disappointments of the last century and a half marks the peak of Edward's achievement as King. As if to demonstrate the vanity of such triumphs the plague returned in 1361 and from then onwards the English hold on French territory was steadily undermined. Delay and incompetence meant that the most important term of the treaty, French acceptance of English sovereignty in Aquitaine, was never ratified. The position was wide open once again. And in 1364 the Dauphin, a very different man from his father, came to the throne as Charles V. He was determined to recover all that had been lost, not in the glory of a great battle, but by steady erosion as English taxation and the indignity of being ruled by Englishmen led the French in Aquitaine to take up arms against their new masters. Castle by castle, town by town, all that the English had won was lost again. English numbers were now too small to hold so great a territory and there was little loot left to attract new adventurers. Many of the great captains were dead and the King's fourth son, John of Gaunt, was a poor military replacement for the ailing Black Prince. By 1374 all that was left was Calais and a coastal strip of south-west France which was smaller than that in English hands at Edward's accession.

Military failure was paralleled at home by a breakdown in the harmony which had been such a characteristic feature of Edward's long reign. The King himself had lost the will to control his kingdom and, as he grew older, sank into a long dotage and increasing dependence on his able but grasping mistress, Alice Perrers. So great a king was still regarded with respect, but popular dislike of the mismanagement of the war and the high taxation which it involved led to increasing criticism of his advisers. The discontent exploded in 1376 with a successful attack by the Commons of the 'Good' Parliament on the King's servants and his mistress who were accused of corruption and peculation. Later that year this unprecedented seizure of initiative by the Commons was reversed and punished by John of Gaunt, now head of the great House of Lancaster, and with the death of his brother the Black Prince in the same year by far the strongest man in the kingdom. Many felt him to be too strong and feared that he planned to disinherit the Black Prince's son, Richard of Bordeaux, and seize the Crown himself at his ageing father's death.

Gaunt's loyalty was soon to be put to the test for Edward III died the following year. His fortunes had sunk low after the glories of the middle years of his reign but the least which could be said for him was that his reign was one of the few half centuries of the later Middle Ages which saw no civil war in England. Unfortunately his recipe for harmony was to leave a dangerous legacy. His policy of curbing aristocratic restlessness by leading the barons to war was to involve England in hostilities for many years to come. And his policy of building up the fortunes of his sons was to create a new generation of over-mighty subjects who would attempt to subdue his grandson, Richard II, just as Thomas of Lancaster had tried to subdue his father.

RICHARD II *r.* 1377-99

N UNEASY HARMONY LAY OVER England when Richard of Bordeaux came to the throne at the age of ten. Court, Commons, Lords and Londoners had played out a somewhat undignified power game as authority slipped from the hands of his ageing grandfather, Edward III, in his long dotage. Umpire of this game had been Richard's eldest uncle, John of Gaunt, unpopular but all-powerful, once suspected of coveting the Crown himself but now apparently the most loyal supporter of his young nephew's hereditary rights. For the next two decades Gaunt lies like a dark shadow over the land, always suspected of ulterior ends, but always in fact a loyal prop to the Crown, a man whose absence from London was a sure harbinger of trouble. Now, in 1377, it was Gaunt, as Steward of England, who organised Richard's coronation, an impressive affair specifically designed to emphasise the sanctity and magnificence of the hereditary monarchy and to usher in a new period of harmony. The chronicler Walsingham described it as 'a day of joy and gladness … the long-awaited day of the renewal of peace and of the laws of the land, long exiled by the weakness of an aged king and the greed of his courtiers and servants'. This was to prove a rather optimistic prediction, since the new King, being a minor, was bound to be weak and there was little likelihood that his courtiers and servants would give up that greed which was the hallmark of their trade. Moreover these were troubled times. Forty years of intermittent warfare had left their mark. Great lords now had large private armies tempered in battle which they were prepared to use against other enemies than France. The country was full of disbanded soldiers skilled in the use of the longbow and keenly aware of its power to lay low the mighty. But the war itself had been going

Er commence le tierc volume des cronicques dengleterre lequel m

badly for a decade. The French celebrated Richard's coronation by raiding the English coast and the people grumbled at the incompetence of their leaders and even more at the mounting cost of that incompetence. Some were soon to go even further and question the assumption that there should be leaders at all. For had not God made all men equal in his own image?

The boy who had just been crowned was to go the furthest of all England's medieval kings in trying to assert the opposite contention – that God had sent the king to rule the people – a belief which was to cost him his life at the age of thirty-three. Perhaps he could have been successful if he had carried the people behind him as a great warrior.

Manuscript illumination from the chronicles of Jean Froissart, showing Richard II, aged ten, holding court after his coronation. Much of his minority was safeguarded by the protection and good counsel of John of Gaunt.

But Richard, son of the Black Prince, inherited only his father's outward appearance and none of his skills at war. Not that he was the coward or weakling of legend – on many occasions in his reign he was to display outstanding courage – but his was the courage of pride, not military prowess.

After his father's death in 1376 the main influences on the young Richard were his gentle and much-loved mother, the thrice-married Joan of Kent, and his tutor, Robert Burley, a knight of his father's household. Soon these influences for moderation and sense were to be overshadowed by his great admiration for his hereditary chamberlain, Robert de Vere, Earl of Oxford, who as the recipient of the King's affection and bounty was to play a part in Richard's reign similar to that of Piers Gaveston in the reign of Edward II. For the moment, however, the influence of the King's court was effectively shackled by the appointment of a regency council chosen specifically so that no one person or group could gain permanent control of policy. Not of the council, but supervising this recipe for weak government, was John of Gaunt.

In 1381 the council was faced with the terrifying challenge of the Peasants' Revolt. This threat to the establishment was extremely well timed. Most of the army was far from London, in Scotland, France or Wales, and John of Gaunt himself was absent in Scotland negotiating a truce. As the two main armies of peasants marched on London from Kent and Essex, there was therefore little readily available force to resist them. The council had no option but to play for time by appeasing the rebels and standing aside as they took their vengeance on those who seemed to be the authors of their grievances. The young King, 'very sad and sorry', shut up in the Tower with his council and watching his city go up in flames from a garret window, makes a pathetic picture. But in reality he was in no personal danger and the watchword of the rebels was 'King Richard and the True Commons'. This misguided faith in the King as the champion of the people against the cruel hand of authority was to last the whole reign.

Richard, still only fourteen, rose to the occasion. With a great company of nobles he rode out to Mile End to meet the rebel spokesman Wat Tyler, face to face. Here he carried out his council's policy of appeasement by consenting to every one of Tyler's demands – the abolition of serfdom, a fixed, low rent for all land, and a general amnesty for the rebels. Satisfied, many of the rebels now went home but a hard core of more desperate men remained. There still seemed to be no plan to disperse the rebels by force. The government's only action was to summon yet another meeting with the rebels.

Here at Smithfield Richard played the most dramatic part of his life. Wat Tyler, puffed up with earlier successes, rode out from the main body of the rebels and in an insulting manner made further demands of the King. But he had gone too far, and the King's retinue attacked and killed him. Realising that they had been betrayed, his supporters began to string their bows, when the young King rode out straight towards the rebels. 'Sirs, will you kill your King?' he cried. 'I am your King, I your captain and your leader. Follow me into the fields.' And the King rode out of the square, followed by the rebels.

The death of Tyler marked the end of the Revolt in London – and ultimately in England. The sheep-like men who had followed their King were rounded up and for the most part sent home. None of the King's promises was fulfilled, though some of the rebels' demands were later implemented by the pressure of economic realities. For the King himself, apart from the huge boost to his reputation, the Revolt had two lessons. The power of deceit in dispersing trouble had been quite clearly demonstrated, and the almost mystical faith of the rebels in their King was later to stir memories in a man who was to have an almost mystical faith in his own ability to rule.

But the King was not yet a ruler and later in the year an attempt was made to bring some more order to his household. Two experienced men, Richard, Earl of Arundel, and Sir Michael de la Pole, were appointed to attend the King and to counsel and govern his person. This sensible move was to have little effect. The King was growing up and, with the encouragement of de Vere, was beginning openly to resent his leading reins. Very soon there developed an almost inevitable polarisation between the immediate court circle and the magnates which was reflected even between the King's two counsellors; de la Pole winning his friendship, while Arundel, whom he had always disliked, became the leading critic of the court.

Such criticism took a familiar form. The court group were monopolising the King's ear and the flow of bounty from the royal office. They were effeminate, preferring love to war, and were indifferent to the prosecution of the struggle against France and Scotland. The King himself did little to win respect. He threw out insults on all sides, on one occasion threatening the Archbishop with his sword and on another telling the Earl of Arundel to go to the devil when he complained of misgovernment. His reputation sank even lower when in 1385 he led the one major military expedition of his reign to Scotland. The result was a fiasco in which the Scots army was never encountered and Richard returned to England after about a fortnight, tired of the whole business. The only factor preventing an open break was the continued presence of John of Gaunt, and Richard had even had a quarrel with him.

In 1386 events moved to a climax when Gaunt sailed from Plymouth to try to make good a claim to the throne of Castile. In his absence the critics of the court moved into action and demanded the dismissal of de la Pole, the Chancellor. Richard's high-handed answer was to say that he would not dismiss a single man from his kitchen at their insistence. But power lay in his critics' hands and a thinly-veiled threat of deposition from their leaders, Arundel and Thomas of Gloucester, the King's youngest uncle, was sufficient. De la Pole was impeached and the government was placed in the hands of a commission of thirteen.

Richard's first instinct was to try to thwart the opposition by getting the impeachment declared illegal and at the same time raising retainers to fight for him if the situation developed into civil war. This advance notice of his intentions brought matters to a head. Late in 1387, Gloucester and Arundel, now joined by the Earl of Warwick, mustered their men to the north of London and forced Richard to agree to the trial of five of his friends, including de Vere and de la Pole, at a Parliament to be held in the New Year. Richard may have agreed, but he did nothing to arrest his friends and de Vere immediately fled to the north-west where he raised an army to impose the King's will on his critics. But to no avail. On 20 December de Vere's army was trapped at Radcot Bridge in Oxfordshire by the forces of the magnates, now augmented by Gaunt's son, Henry Bolingbroke, and Thomas Mowbray, Earl of Nottingham. De Vere escaped in the mist to die in exile, but others of the King's friends were not so lucky and now had to face the vengeance of their victorious critics.

The Merciless Parliament of 1388 was dominated by the five Lords Appellant, as the leaders of the opposition were called, who, dressed in golden surcoats, led a full-scale attack on the King's household. Those of their original five victims who had not fled suffered the hideous penalties for treason and this fate was shared by other members of the court party, including the King's old tutor, Sir Robert Burley. The King was stunned by this judicial murder of his friends. There was little he could do but obey the Lords Appellant, now the real sovereigns of the land, but it is clear that for the rest of his reign his deepest wish was to avenge himself for his loss. He was, however, quite prepared to take his time.

The first move came in the following year when the King, now aged twenty-two, announced his intention to rule as a monarch of full age. No one could query his right to do so and indeed the King made no attempt at this stage to be provocative. Minor changes were made in the household but there was no victimisation and the King went out of his way to be friendly with the Appellants. A further sign of the return to normality came with the arrival of John of Gaunt back from Spain. This atmosphere of peace was to last for six years.

During this period the statesman Richard had some success. In 1394 he scored a triumph by bringing a settlement to anarchic Ireland and in 1396 concluded a very successful twenty-eight years' truce with France.

As the quiet years passed by, Richard was surreptitiously building up his power as King. The most obvious illustration of this was in his creation of a magnificent court, designed to soothe the great and to impress his lesser subjects with his own regality. It was rather different from previous English courts and owed much to continental example, partly as a result of Richard's two foreign marriages, to Anne of Bohemia in 1382 and after her death in 1394 to Isabella of France. Earlier English courts had tended to be geared to war; Richard's court was more peaceful, and although the knightly ideals remained, they tended to be more those of the courtly knight than of the knight in the field. Presiding over everything was an increasingly flamboyant and dilettante king.

There was nothing dilettante about Richard's activities outside the court, however. For while faction was hushed in luxury at court, Richard was preparing for future trouble by recruiting in Ireland, Wales and Cheshire a substantial private army which received his pay and wore his famous badge of the white hart.

In 1397 he was ready to strike. Without warning, Gloucester, Arundel and Warwick were arrested, Gloucester being sent to Calais where he was quietly strangled. In September Richard's old enemies were tried before Parliament in a deliberate parody of the Merciless Parliament. Arundel was executed, but Warwick, who pleased the King greatly by making an abject confession of his guilt, was banished for life to the Isle of Man. Now it was the turn of the two younger Appellants, Bolingbroke and Mowbray, to fear for their safety. Both of them had recently been the recipients of the King's favour but they must have been uneasy. In 1398 Mowbray confided his uneasiness to Bolingbroke

Following pages: The Wilton Diptych, showing Richard II kneeling before the Virgin. He is being presented by St Edmund (king and martyr), St Edward the Confessor and St John the Baptist, and round his neck is the white hart insignia that he adopted in 1390. The angels are wearing his insignia too.

and the latter, on the advice of his father, John of Gaunt, reported Mowbray's treasonable remarks to the King. Mowbray stoutly denied the accusation of treason and, since there had been no witnesses to the conversation, it was decided that the truth could only be determined by trial by combat. For Richard it seemed a god-sent opportunity to rid himself of the last two of his old enemies at one go. Elaborate preparations had been made for such an exciting contest and the battle was just about to begin, when Richard in the most dramatic way stopped the combat and exiled both the contestants, Bolingbroke for ten years and Mowbray for life.

Now Richard was free to act as he liked. With his enemies dead or in exile and with a large private army at his command, he began to demonstrate the powers of an absolute king. Those who offended him were forced to purchase pardons at a high price. Arbitrary taxes were demanded. The records of Parliament were altered to condemn his enemies as traitors. The rule of law was overridden. Richard himself took on megalomaniac airs, spending recklessly and building a great throne from which on feast-days he could look down on his guests – any who caught his eye being forced to kneel to his majesty. Hatred of the King's Cheshire archers and fear of his power were widespread but there was little that anyone could do. Armed power was controlled by the King and by a group mainly of his kinsmen who had been rewarded with the forfeit estates of Arundel and Gloucester.

In February 1399 John of Gaunt died. In his last years he had been once again a loyal prop to Richard; as Steward he had been in the forefront of the procedure which led to the destruction of Gloucester, Arundel and Warwick, and when in turn his own son was banished he had said not a word. Gaunt's death would have been a good opportunity to pardon his son and maintain the power of Lancaster as a support to the Crown. Instead Richard took the step which was to lead to the rapid curtailment of his arbitrary exercise of power. Bolingbroke's exile was increased to life and his inheritance was seized. No longer could any magnate feel secure in possession of his lands and the determination of the lords to resist the King now only awaited a leader.

Richard was still sublimely confident of his power and that summer he set off to Ireland where the settlement of 1394 had once more dissolved into rebellion. With him he took nearly all his supporters, leaving behind his last remaining uncle, the incompetent Edmund of York, as keeper of the realm. A few weeks later Bolingbroke sailed from Boulogne to claim his inheritance. As he made his triumphal progress from Ravenspur on the Humber across the middle of England, all resistance disappeared and his small number of followers was soon swollen by the retinues of lords eager to greet him. Richard's Cheshire archers, whose arrogance and depredations had been the prop of his power, slunk off to their homes, stripping off their white hart badges as they went. Richard himself, whose personal courage had never been in doubt, left Ireland for the region in which he had most personal support, North Wales. It was a hopeless mission. Betrayed and deserted, he soon found himself a prisoner of Bolingbroke in the Tower, later to be removed to the fatal safety of Lancastrian Pontefract.

So successful had Bolingbroke's enterprise been that he decided himself to seize the throne. The precedent of 1327 could be used to depose King Richard, though he proved more difficult to coerce into abdicating than Edward II. Somewhat more tricky was the fact that Bolingbroke was not the heir of the childless Richard, whose most plausible successor was the eight-year-old Earl of March. But this was no time for a minor, and after much debate Bolingbroke successfully challenged the Crown, 'through the right that God of his grace hath sent me, with the help of my kin and of my friends'. Richard, like Edward II, was now too dangerous to live, a fact which was made self-evident when on Twelfth Night 1400, a group of Richard's friends tried to murder Henry IV and all his family preparatory to restoring their captive King. So Richard was secretly murdered in Pontefract Castle and for the rest of his life Henry IV was to be haunted by guilt and doubt – guilt for the murder of an anointed king, and doubt on the part of interested persons that Richard was really dead. It was left for Henry V to lay the bogy for ever when, secure in his Lancastrian inheritance, he removed the remains of the murdered King from their inglorious resting place to the tomb that Richard had built for himself in Westminster Abbey.

INDEX

PICTURE CREDITS

theartarchive: endpapers, pages 14, 21, 34
The Bridgeman Art Library, London: pages 2, 17, 40, 45, 94, 104-105, 109
Weidenfeld & Nicolson Archives: pages 8, 51, 58, 62, 69, 76, 89, 90, 91, 99
Topham Picturepoint: pages 13, 26, 33, 43, 57, 60, 73, 85
British Library: pages 25, 31
AKG London: pages 48, 55, 114-115
Hulton Getty: page 52
Dean & Chapter of Westminster: page 77
National Monuments Record, RCHME: page 79
Woodmansterne: page 80
Conway Library, Coutauld Institute of Art: page 97